Gemstone

Tumbling, Cutting, Drilling & Cabochon Making

Jim Magnuson with **Val Carver**
Photography by Carol Wood

Adventure Publications
Cambridge, Minnesota

Dedication

In memorial to my father and mother, who unknowingly gave me a great love for working with my hands and a great love of rocks. I guess it was inevitable that I became a lapidary artist and teacher.

—With great love and respect, *Val Brubaker Carver*

We would like to thank our sister Ann O'Keefe for her continued partnership in our book-making adventures.

—*Jim Magnuson* and *Carol Wood*

Cover and book design by Jonathan Norberg
Edited by Dan Downing
All photos by Carol Wood

10 9 8 7 6

Gemstone Tumbling, Cutting, Drilling & Cabochon Making
Copyright © 2015 by Jim Magnuson
Published by Adventure Publication
An imprint of AdventureKEEN
310 Garfield Street South
Cambridge, Minnesota 55008
(800) 678-7006
www.adventurepublications.net
All rights reserved
Printed in China
ISBN 978-1-59193-460-8 (pbk.); ISBN 978-1-59193-535-3 (ebook)

Gemstone

Tumbling, Cutting, Drilling & Cabochon Making

Table of Contents

The Lapidary Arts

If you have ever marveled at beautifully cut, polished and shaped gemstones and wondered what it would take to create your own, you might be surprised at how quickly you can learn how to do it! With a little focused instruction and today's advanced tools and equipment, you can discover the rewarding experience of taking rough stones and making your own creations. And you'll be pleased to learn that creating finished gemstones is quite afford-able, especially when compared with many other popular hobbies.

There are numerous books and online articles and videos about cutting, polishing and drilling gemstones and making them into cabochons, which are shaped, domed and polished stones commonly used in jewelry. (Taken together, these processes are generally referred to as the lapidary arts.) So why create another lapidary book? Unfortunately, most of the material that is currently available is badly out of date or irrelevant to today's readers. Worse yet, older books don't provide the high-quality, full-color images that hobbyists need to learn lapidary processes. Additionally, none of the existing publications provide up-to-date information about the costs of lapidary machinery and the tools and supplies needed for each lapidary process. And finally, there is no single guidebook that comprehensively covers each of the different lapidary processes from start to finish. This often leaves the user guessing about how everything fits together.

You might also wonder why you shouldn't just skip ahead to the internet and look for instructional videos on YouTube. We whole-heartedly endorse supplementing your learning with online video clips, but only after you have gained an understanding of the different tools and processes you'll be using to create lapidary products. You will get several additional things in this book that you will not get from a set of random video clips:

1) Recommendations on lapidary machines, in terms of machine types, makes and models, and approximate prices of the different machine types, as well as additional supplies and materials needed for lapidary work.

2) Reference charts that help you pull together information on how to go about different projects—starting from the very beginning, with knowing the types of gemstones to use.

3) Simple, easy-to-follow directions that are complemented by action-oriented photos that clearly represent the simplest and most reliable way to perform key lapidary operations. Along the way, we show you how a project progresses from a rough stone to a finished product, helping you visualize the transformation of raw gemstone to lapidary artwork.

4) Helpful tips, charts and checklists to jump-start your learning, help you overcome the fear of getting started, and help you stay efficient, all while simultaneously helping you keep costs down. These tools will help beginners achieve success quickly and make the best use of precious time, gemstones and lapidary supplies. They will also be useful as reference charts for years to come, and they can be adapted to your own preferences and experiences.

5) And perhaps the most helpful aspect of this book is that in addition to covering lapidary processes and the equipment necessary to perform them, we show how these techniques and tools relate to each other, and how they work together to take you from start to finish.

Our goal with this book is to provide a one-stop shop for beginners and for others who have recently started their lapidary journey. Some of you may have tried out a lapidary process, such as tumbling, only to get frustrated and quit altogether. We'll help you avoid that. We have intentionally left out the most complex and costly lapidary methods and machines, such as commercial equipment and "combination machines" (arbor and trim saw combinations, for example). Similarly, including complex wire wrapping and jewelry setting is likely to frustrate the beginner, as it takes a good deal of skill and practice, so instead we've included some basic styles and techniques that you can easily modify to create your own designs. (For those looking for more advanced instruction, see Recommended Reading for Jewelry Making on page 170.) We also don't include information about rock breaking or rough slab sawing of very large pieces of stone, such as oversized chunks of jasper or petrified wood (smaller pieces of these materials are fine), because the equipment required is quite costly, and it's easy to obtain pre-cut slabs from lapidary stores. And lastly, we don't cover how to produce spheres or marbles, as this equipment is more specialized and expensive.

Instead, this book will keep it simple and cover a variety of the most popular lapidary arts, helping you produce high-quality gemstone products that you will be proud to display, wear or even sell!

aventurine

agua nueva agate

labradorite

Lake Superior agate

polka dot agate

jasper with agate

rose quartz

Apache tear

Brazilian agate

petrified wood

Willow Creek jasper

blue lace agate

paua shell

tiger eye

malachite

moonstone

picture jasper

petrified palm wood

jasper

dino bone

rhodonite

Laguna agate

moss agate

mother of pearl

lapis lazuli

African queen picture jasper

turquoise

Botswana agate

Mexican crazy lace agate

snowflake obsidian

Materials, Machines and Finished Products

In this chapter, we'll cover the basics of gemstone materials, the types of lapidary products you can make from them and the general process steps and lapidary machines you need to know about.

Most hobbyists start with the simplest projects and work their way up, but others have a specific goal in mind, like making jewelry, and therefore they want to quickly learn each of the necessary operations. Regardless of where you fit in this spectrum, keep in mind that lapidary supply stores can provide you with gemstones that have been partially processed, which allows you to jump in wherever you are comfortable or most interested.

Gemstone Materials Commonly Used in Lapidary Work

Not all stones are suitable for performing lapidary arts, and there are some that are quite difficult to work with, so in this book we focus on a variety of accessible and affordable stones that you can turn into beautiful showpieces and jewelry. To work a stone, it must be hard enough to be cut, shaped and polished. The Mohs hardness scale is used to express the hardness of different minerals, with a hardness of 1 being the softest (talc has a hardness of 1) and 10 being the hardest (diamonds are a 10). The majority of stones that we recommend are in the 6-7 range; examples include agate, jasper and turquoise. There is an endless variety of colors and patterns in the gemstones we recommend, so they should be more than suitable for whatever project you want to complete. On occasion, these gemstones differ in hardness; when this affects a lapidary process, we'll give you tips on how to work such a stone.

In addition to selecting the types of gemstones that you want to use, take the time to choose stones with pleasing colors and patterns. The saying "garbage in = garbage out" is nowhere more true than in the lapidary arts—in fact, we have adapted the saying specifically to lapidary work: garbage in = shiny garbage out. All of your fine work cutting and polishing will be wasted on poor-quality stones. This doesn't mean that you need to spend a fortune on acquiring expensive raw materials, because the types of stones we are recommending can be obtained at reasonable prices, and you can even find them on your own rockhounding adventures! That being said, if you are just a beginner, it's perfectly acceptable, and in fact advisable, to use (and learn on) lower quality stones.

What You Can Do with Your Gemstone Materials

Once you have selected a few stones that you'd like to work with, it's time to decide what to do with them. There are many different ways to use your gemstones. You can polish the whole stones in a tumbler, you can polish just a portion of the stone (its "face") or you can prepare your gemstones for use in jewelry. If you're planning on using them in jewelry, you can use the whole stones in one piece, slice them and use sections in your jewelry pieces, or use them to create a cabochon, which is a shaped, domed and polished stone commonly used in jewelry. Below are some examples of the lapidary products we'll be teaching you how to make, with reference to the lapidary processes used to make them.

PRODUCT	DESCRIPTION
Tumble-polished whole stones for display	Gemstones that have been fully polished on all sides of the stone; these are usually displayed in glass bowls and jars and make nice eye candy displays
Tumble-polished whole stones for use in jewelry	Tumble-polished whole stones can be face drilled (through the stone) or top drilled (into the top), with the holes used to attach a jewelry finding; they can also be wire wrapped
Natural-shape cut-stone pendants for use in jewelry	Whole gemstones that have been cut into jewelry pendant slabs and left in the natural shape of the whole stone; pendants are tumble polished and then wire wrapped with copper, bronze, silver or gold wrapping wire; wrapping designs can range from simple to elaborate; pendants can also be either face drilled or top drilled, with the holes used to attach a jewelry finding
Cabochon stone pendants for use in jewelry	Stones that have been cut into thin slabs or slices, then cut and shaped into ovals, circles, squares or other shapes and then placed into a jewelry setting; cabochons can be face drilled or top drilled, with the holes used to attach a jewelry finding; they can also be wire wrapped
Face-polished or dome-polished stones	The most beautiful face of a larger-size whole stone is polished; this showcases the beautiful color and pattern on the polished face and the natural formation of the rough, unfinished sides

tumble-polished whole stone

natural-shape cut stone

cabochon stone pendant

face-polished stone

13

Lapidary Machines

To create the lapidary products we discuss, you will need specific lapidary machines, tools and lapidary supplies. Because this book is about demystifying the process for beginners, we will provide detailed information about machinery and specific recommendations to get you started quickly.

Machine Definitions and Uses

- **Tumblers** are enclosed, hardened rubber barrels that either rotate (rotary tumblers) or vibrate (vibratory tumblers) and gradually smooth and polish your gemstones

- **Lapidary drill presses** are similar to drill presses made for drilling into metal or wood, but they operate at lower speeds and spray cooling fluids onto stones; drill presses can be used either to drill all the way through a stone (face drilling) or into the top of a stone (top drilling)

- **Trim saws** are used to cut away broken "faces" from gemstones (so they can be face polished), to cut gemstone materials into slabs or slices and to trim rough slabs or slices into shaped jewelry pendants, known as cabochons

- **Dop pots** are for heating up dopping wax, which is used to securely fasten a gemstone to a dop stick; this helps give you a firm hold on your gemstones as you grind and polish them

- **Flat lapidary sanders** are used to grind, sand and polish one side or "face" of a jewelry pendant or whole stone that is being face or dome polished

- **Routers** are used to create a shallow groove around the edge of a jewelry pendant stone; a thin wire or cord is fit into the groove and then attached to a necklace or bracelet

PRODUCT	LAPIDARY MACHINES REQUIRED
Tumble-polished whole stones	A rotary or vibratory tumbler
Tumble-polished whole stones used in jewelry	A rotary or vibratory tumbler and a lapidary drill press (a drill press isn't needed if stones will be wire wrapped)
Natural-shape cut-stone pendants used in jewelry*	A rotary or vibratory tumbler, a trim saw and a lapidary drill press (a drill press isn't needed if stones will be wire wrapped)
Cabochons or shaped stone pendants used in jewelry	A rotary or vibratory tumbler, a trim saw, a flat lapidary sander, a dop pot and a lapidary drill press (a drill press isn't needed if stones will be wire wrapped or placed in a jewelry setting)
Face- or dome-polished stones	A flat lapidary sander and a trim saw (optional)

*In a natural-shape pendant, slices are cut from a whole stone (such as a Lake Superior agate) and are left in the shape of the stone.

Lapidary Machine and Supply Pricing

Listed below are current prices for some of the lapidary equipment and supplies needed to perform each lapidary process. These prices are representative of what you might find at a full-service lapidary supply store. Prices are estimates and will vary over time. In addition to the brands of machines listed, the names of other quality machine manufacturers are provided in the chapter about each process; they are also listed on page 171.

Tumble Polishing

Lortone 3-lb. rotary tumbler	$96
Lortone 12-lb. rotary tumbler	$220
Lot-O Tumbler 4.5-lb. vibratory tumbler	$210
Coarse grit (60–80 mesh) - 1 lb.	$5
Medium grit (180–220 mesh) - 1 lb.	$5
Fine grit (500 mesh) - 1 lb.	$8
Aluminum oxide polish - 1 lb.	$9
Ceramic tumbling media - 1 lb.	$7

Sawing

High-Tech Diamond 6" saw	$439
Lortone 8" saw	$680
Diamond sintered 6" blade	$58
Diamond sintered 8" blade	$74
Rockhound saw oil - 1 gal.	$24
Rock saw dressing stick	$20

Face Polishing

Ameritool 8" lapidary sander	$400
5-disc lapidary sander set	$334
Ultra-coarse grinding disc	$100
Diamond polishing paste - 10 g	$16
Diamond extender fluid - 2 oz.	$6
Diamond extender spray - 2 oz.	$15

Routing

Gryphon Gryphette router	$81
Router bit for grooving	$14
Other router bits	$14

Drilling

Micro-Mark drill and coolant system	$424
Hollow-core diamond drill bits (set of 6)	$22
Coolant fluid - 8 oz.	$8
Coolant spray nozzles (set of 6)	$9

Cabochon Making

Dop pot	$36
Dop wax (4 sticks)	$18
Cabochon double stencils (set of 3)	$48
Dop sticks (12)	$4
Wire wrapping tool set	$60

A Few More Suggestions

Get acquainted with a well-established lapidary supply shop. If you are lucky, there will be one within driving distance and you can visit the shop in person; otherwise you should find one through online research and establish a relationship. There are also many jewelry and beading stores that offer classes on jewelry making, which may include instruction in the related lapidary processes. While you may be able to save money by shopping online for the lowest price on a given piece of equipment, you will be glad to have the advice of an expert when something isn't going as expected or a machine is not functioning properly, and it's nice to get tips on new tools, processes and lapidary supplies. Some shops even create specially adapted equipment that will streamline or simplify processes even more than we describe in this book. Through this relationship you will probably also get to know other amateur lapidary artists in your area that you can share your ideas and creations with.

We also urge you to find a local rock and mineral club and join it! Every club has a few true lapidary artists, and almost invariably they will generously offer their time and patient advice. Getting hands-on practice with someone who has learned the tricks of the trade is invaluable. These lapidary veterans may also show you other methods that better suit your personal style. So join a club and find a comfortable place to learn and share as your own skills continue to improve.

And when it comes to lapidary work, one last thing to keep in mind is that everyone has their own personal style and preferences. As your skills improve, your own interests will grow and evolve as you are introduced to the incredibly diverse world of gemstone cutting, polishing and jewelry making!

Gemstones Types and Lapidary Uses

Now that you've got a general introduction to the types of gemstone material best suited for beginner-to-intermediate lapidary hobbyists and artists, we'll show you which gemstones are best for specific types of lapidary work.

Not all gemstones can be used in the same way. For example, some gemstones are too large to be tumble polished or face polished as individual stones. If you want to polish such specimens, they must first be cut into slabs and then shaped into jewelry pieces. The chart on page 21 provides general recommendations for the types of lapidary products that can be produced with each gemstone. While this chart is by no means exhaustive, the lapidary materials that we recommend provide a broad cross section of the gemstone types that are readily available, affordable, and that lend themselves well to beginning and intermediate lapidary artwork. Most importantly, you can use them to produce outstanding finished stones and jewelry pieces.

Gemstone Prices

Most of the stones we recommend in this book can be purchased in bulk and are priced by the pound. The low end of the price range is about $3–5 per pound, medium-level stones are $8–15 per pound, and high-priced stones go for over $20 per pound. As you gain skill and confidence, you may choose to move up this scale, but rest assured, you can produce many delightful lapidary products with carefully selected gemstones from the low end of this price range.

Selecting High-Quality Gemstones

Once you know which gemstone you want to use, and how you want to use it, you have to be able to recognize high-quality specimens to purchase. Just as choosing lousy produce at the grocery store will get you a sub-par dinner, the same concept applies when it comes to lapidary work: garbage in = shiny garbage out. While it will certainly take time for you to consistently achieve high-quality results, starting with high-quality stones is the best way to avoid frustration.

HELPFUL TIP: In some cases higher-grade stones are available, but they can be expensive; if you're a beginner at the lapidary arts, these are not your best bet, as there is more to lose if you accidentally damage them.

GEMSTONE TYPES	COST	TUMBLE POLISHED WHOLE STONES	FACE/DOME POLISHED STONES	NATURAL SHAPE JEWELRY PENDANTS	SHAPED JEWELRY STONES/ CABOCHONS
Lake Superior Agate	$$–$$$	Yes	Yes	Yes	Yes
Brazilian Agate	$–$$	Yes	Yes	Yes	Yes
Prairie Agate	$	Yes	Yes	Yes	Yes
Laguna Agate	$$–$$$	No	Yes	Yes	Yes
Botswana Agate	$$–$$$	Yes	Yes	Yes	Yes
Crazy Lace Agate	$$–$$$	No	Yes	No	Yes
Bubblegum Agate	$	Yes	No	Yes	No
Montana Moss Agate	$–$$$	No	Yes	No	Yes
Green Tree Agate	$$	No	No	Yes	Yes
Blue Lace Agate	$$	Yes	Yes	Yes	Yes
Tiger Eye	$$	Yes	No	No	Yes
Rhodonite	$$	Yes	No	No	Yes
Binghamite	$$	No	No	No	Yes
Aventurine	$$	Yes	No	No	Yes
Sodalite	$–$$	Yes	No	No	Yes
Lapis Lazuli	$$–$$$	Yes	No	No	Yes
Jade	$$–$$$	Yes	No	No	Yes
Smoky Quartz	$$–$$$	Yes	No	No	Yes
Rose Quartz	$$–$$$	Yes	No	No	Yes
Amethyst Quartz	$–$$	Yes	No	No	Yes
Clear Quartz	$$$	Yes	No	No	Yes
Banded Jasper	$	Yes	No	No	Yes
Mary Ellen Jasper	$	Yes	No	No	Yes
Ocean Jasper	$$–$$$	Yes	No	No	Yes
Picture Jasper	$$–$$$	Yes	No	No	Yes
Petrified Wood (many types)	$–$$	Yes	Yes	No	Yes
Turquoise	$$–$$$	No	No	Yes	Yes
Moonstone	$$–$$$	No	No	Yes	Yes
Apache Tears	$	Yes	No	No	Yes
Obsidian (many types)	$	Yes	No	No	Yes
Sea Glass	$	Yes	No	No	No

$=$3–5 per pound
$$=$8–15 per pound
$$$=over $20 per pound

HELPFUL TIP: When we recommend against using a specific type of stone for a given project, it doesn't necessarily mean it's impossible. In some cases it can work, but it will likely take some additional work and may not be the best use for the given type of stone.

Binghamite

below lapidary grade   medium grade   lapidary grade

Blue Lace Agate

below lapidary grade   medium grade   lapidary grade

Green Tree Agate

below lapidary grade   medium grade   lapidary grade

A Visual Guide to Selecting Gemstones

To give you an idea of where to start, we've selected a number of gemstones listed in the chart on page 21 to discuss in further detail and help you select high-quality materials. While we don't do this with every mineral or gemstone in the chart, those that we include are good stand-ins for a number of others, and the same selection tips apply to them as well. To make things as intuitive as possible, on pages 24–41 we've provided four photos for each type of gemstone material shown: one of rough stones that are below lapidary grade, one of rough stones that we consider lapidary grade, an image showing cut slabs, and a photo of a completed lapidary piece ready for jewelry making. This combination of images will help demystify this part of the lapidary process.

As their name suggests, below-grade stones don't warrant the effort and cost necessary for them to serve as display stones or jewelry pieces. In contrast, lapidary-grade stones represent the sweet spot for most of your lapidary products. For stones that contain patterns or banding (such as agates, jaspers, or petrified wood), the primary characteristics you're looking for are brightness and intensity of color, color separation (including distinctive layering or banding patterns), deep banding patterns and unique coloration. When it comes to non-banded stones (quartz varieties, obsidian, aventurine), lower-quality stones are milkier or dull in color, while higher-quality stones are purer, less fractured and brightly or uniquely colored.

Lake Superior Agate

Below-grade Lake Superior Agates show almost no visible pattern and are not worth the investment for tumbling and jewelry making. Note, however, that Lake Superior agates sometimes require an "exploratory cut" to determine whether the banding patterns and colors are of lapidary quality.

Lapidary-grade Lake Superior Agates show nice color variations and some banding patterns; the stones pictured would make nice jewelry pieces or tumble-polished stones for display.

Cut slabs and finished stones: Here you can see cut slabs, as well as polished natural-shape slabs and a nicely finished cabochon. If you use small, whole stones, the finished products have unique, natural shapes that you can incorporate in jewelry.

Gemstone types that follow the same grading and selection rules: Botswana agate, Laguna agate, Brazilian agate, prairie agate, blue lace agate

Crazy Lace Agate

Below-grade Crazy Lace Agates have very little banding pattern visible on the exterior, though it's usually worth cutting a stone in half to see if there is more pattern on the interior of the stone.

Lapidary-grade Crazy Lace Agates have superb visible banding patterns; once the stones have been cut into slabs, they will offer several nice options for cabochon shapes.

Cut slabs and finished stones: Shown above are slabs with excellent banding plus crazy lace agate's signature patterns and colors. When you're deciding how to use this gemstone for lapidary work, you might go crazy deciding where exactly to mark your stencil lines and saw cuts, since there will be lots of choices! Below are some beautiful crazy lace agate cabochons. There are some lapidary artists that specialize in making very high-end crazy lace jewelry pieces, and given how good the agates look, you can see why.

Gemstone types that follow the same grading and selection rules: Blue lace agate and other gemstone materials that must be cut into slabs for lapidary work follow the same general selection guidelines.

Picture Jasper

Below-grade Picture Jasper specimens are almost indistinguishable—you can hardly recognize what they are except for a few glimpses of the signature colors. The chunk shown above will not warrant your time or effort.

Lapidary-grade Picture Jasper is brightly colored and shows a good deal of contrast and pattern variation. This specimen will produce numerous slabs that can be cut into cabochons, with nicely highlighted color variations.

Cut slabs and finished stones: Cut slabs really highlight picture jasper's namesake "picture" patterning, which is intricate and absolutely stunning. You might have a hard time cutting this stone into one or more cabochons since it is so beautiful as is. When picture jasper is cut into cabochons, the pieces illustrate the intense shine and polish that can be obtained from this gemstone material, and their soft colors make for outstanding jewelry pieces.

Gemstone types that follow the same grading and selection rules: Almost all jaspers follow the guidelines for picture jasper.

Lapis Lazuli

Below-grade Lapis Lazuli stones have material with a chalky white matrix, and they lack the striking deep-blue coloration found in higher-quality gemstone material.

Lapidary-grade Lapis Lazuli stones have both a deep-blue coloration and the prized gold-colored matrix ingrained within the stone. This golden coloration occurs because of pyrite mineral inclusions and impurities.

Cut slabs and finished stones: Lapis lazuli slabs have a striking blue-and-gold color scheme that will yield the shimmering qualities that this gemstone is prized for. When used in cabochons, you can achieve a range of colors. One of the cabochons shown below has more of the gold matrix banding, whereas the other has a sparkle effect that comes from calcite or mica inclusions and impurities.

Gemstone types that follow the same grading and selection rules: Lapis lazuli is similar in many respects to sodalite and aventurine. Note that lapis lazuli can be pricey. If the price is too high for you, sodalite is a great lower-priced substitute; high-quality stones exhibit color variations that are similar to those found in lapis.

Tiger Eye

Below-grade Tiger Eye stones are brownish and lack the brighter gold coloration and iridescence of higher-grade pieces.

Lapidary-grade Tiger Eye shows a beautiful section of tiger eye pattern. Replete with striking lines and bright colors, it will almost certainly yield high-quality slabs. However, when it comes to tiger eye, we strongly recommend that beginners buy pre-cut slabs that show contrasting color bands. It takes time to learn how to cut tiger eye to produce the best lapidary specimens.

Cut slabs and finished stones: These pre-cut slabs show off the golden- and deep-brown color variations that make tiger eye famous. The cabochon below is absolutely first class, with striking color variations and iridescence.

Gemstone types that follow the same grading and selection rules: Binghamite follows the same guidelines; it isn't referred to as "Minnesota tiger eye" for nothing.

Rose Quartz

Below-grade Rose Quartz stones are dull in color, milky and highly fractured. The stone shown above could possibly be broken or cut into stones for tumble polishing or beadwork, but given its low quality, it wouldn't be suitable for jewelry making.

Lapidary-grade Rose Quartz stones exhibit a beautiful and vibrant rose color and are almost glassy in their clarity.

Cut slabs and finished stones: The cut slab above is ideal for making multiple cabochons. Rose quartz and other quartz varieties are also ideal for making three-dimensional shapes, such as hearts, cubes and spheres. Note, however, that making these may require a higher skill level or special machines not covered in this book. The rose quartz cabochon below shows just how beautiful this material can look when finished.

Gemstone types that follow the same grading and selection rules: All quartz varieties, including amethyst, smoky quartz and clear quartz.

35

Obsidian

Below-grade Obsidian stones are dull gray and have neither the glassy luster or color variability of higher-quality materials.

Lapidary-grade Obsidian stones are glassy and show hints of nice color variations that may be revealed when cut into slabs. Like some other gemstones, you will discover more about the quality of the stone as you cut into successive layers.

Cut slabs and finished stones: The cut slab above is a stunning piece of mahogany obsidian and features some fiery color that almost seems to glow. This is a beautiful display piece in its own right, but it would make premium cabochon and jewelry pieces, like the beautiful high-gloss cabochon below.

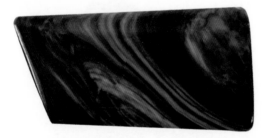

Gemstone types that follow the same grading and selection rules: Petrified wood is similar when it comes to pattern and color variation, and when you're selecting quartz varieties, use obsidian as your guide for judging clarity.

Aventurine

Below-grade Aventurine stones often consist of chalky white chunks; these are unworthy of lapidary work.

Lapidary-grade Aventurine shows more of its characteristic green shading and is more translucent, making it well suited for cutting into slabs.

Cut slabs and finished stones: The deep-green cut slab shown above-right is of an incredibly high quality and will yield stunning jewelry pieces. The other slab, while not as vibrant, is also a high-quality piece. The cabochon below is a nice deep green with alternating bands of white. This piece shows the importance of the placement of your cabochon stencils, with the angled color lines making for a more interesting display.

Gemstone types that follow the same grading and selection rules: Aventurine is similar in most respects to quartz, sodalite and lapis lazuli.

Petrified Wood

Below-grade Petrified Wood pieces are often a dull gray; while such specimens are still interesting, they are probably best suited for a rock garden, aquarium or other similar type of display.

Lapidary-grade Petrified Wood exhibits its characteristic wood-grain pattern. Even if a stone shows wood-grain patterning, making an exploratory cut is often worthwhile, as it allows you to see if the interior pattern is better suited for tumble polishing or making cabochons.

Cut slabs and finished stones: The slab shown above is incredibly intense and would likely leave you wondering whether to cut it into cabs or leave it as is. For example, there are numerous sections in the slab that would lend well to cutting, either by using a stencil or creating free-form shapes. The two cabochons shown below illustrate the amazing diversity found in petrified wood varieties. Just as with agates, there are innumerable types of petrified wood varieties found around the world.

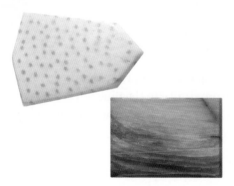

Gemstone types that follow the same grading and selection rules: Oddly enough, some types of obsidian can be confused with petrified wood, and choosing them is similar to selecting obsidian specimens.

Turquoise

For Turquoise, rather than differentiating the stones as lapidary grade or below-lapidary grade, we chose to highlight a few specimens that show different characteristics unique to the mines that they originated from. Turquoise is a highly sought-after gemstone material and is found in several geographies around the world. The three types that we show are all from the Desert Southwest region of the United States, primarily Nevada. Turquoise is often fashioned into intricate jewelry pieces after being cut, shaped and polished. It is a softer gemstone material, and as such it requires lighter handling in grinding, tumbling and polishing operations.

Blue Moon Turquoise comes from a mine in Candelaria Hills that's in close proximity to the Blue Boy Mine, near Coaldale, Nevada. Blue moon turquoise features light- to medium-blue hues, with some deeper blue, high-grade materials.

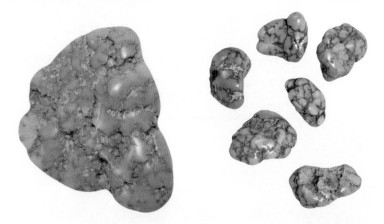

Godber Turquoise comes from a well-known Nevada mine that has produced some very high-grade stones. Godber Turquoise specimens contain deep-blue to green colorations and feature a spider web matrix.

Fox Turquoise comes from the Fox Mine, which is famous for its productivity and is part of a series of mines from the Cortez land claims. Turquoise specimens from the Fox Mine include a range of blue-green, blue and green colorations, with an occasional spider-web matrix.

Tumble Polishing

What It Is

Gemstones are gently rolled or vibrated until they reach either a high-gloss or a satin (semi-gloss) finish.

Process Overview

Tumbling involves several cycles of loading the tumbler barrel (drum) with stones, tumbling media and grinding or polishing compounds until the desired finish is achieved.

Equipment and Lapidary Supplies

Tumbling requires a rock tumbler. There are two primary tumbling machine options. A rotary tumbler is best for removing jagged edges and producing more rounded stones, but it takes up to six times as long as a vibratory tumbler. Vibratory tumblers are fast, efficient, and gentler on your stones, but they make a bit more noise and need more regular attention. Both machines use silicon carbide abrasives (grits) for grinding and aluminum oxide polishing compounds.

Process Highlights

Tumbling is a relatively straightforward and repetitive process that proceeds through multiple tumbling stages. Thorough and patient cleaning of stones between stages is the best recipe for success.

Time Requirements

Rotary tumbling takes 33 days for a high-gloss polish and 25 days for a satin finish. Vibratory tumblers take 6 days for high-gloss and 3 days for a satin finish.

3-lb. rotary tumbler

12-lb. rotary tumbler

4.5-lb. vibratory tumbler

Recommended Equipment

There are dozens of makes, models, sizes and types of tumblers. Generally speaking, however, there are two major kinds of tumblers—rotary and vibratory. There are major differences in what they do, how you use them, and the overall results you can expect. Most amateur hobbyists will pick one machine over the other, while others may have one of each.

In this book, we only focus on a few specific machines, because they are proven and are usually the amateur lapidary artists' machines of choice. While these "select few" are not the only machines that can produce high-quality results, we know that these machines do. They are also both affordable and reliable and will produce many years of use and enjoyment. We also want to remind you that lower price machines can be a recipe for frustration and might lead you to give up on tumble polishing your gemstones.

Two recommended tumbler brands are Lortone and Lot-O Tumbler (shown above). Other quality tumbler brands are Thumler's Tumbler, Diamond Pacific and Covington Engineering. Regardless of which make or model you purchase, we strongly recommend one with a hardened rubber barrel. These models are quieter than those with plastic barrels. Plastic barrels also often become contaminated with abrasives, resulting in poor-quality polishing.

Rotary Tumbler Advantages

- Cheaper initial cost ($100 for a small rotary vs. $200 for a small vibratory)

- Quieter; it sounds almost like a small brook, with water running over the stones in the streambed

- Removes more stone when needed, such as with very rough stones, or stones that you wish to have a more rounded shape

- Being able to turn it on and walk away for 10-20 days gives the perception of lower maintenance, but it's about the same effort in the long run as a vibratory tumbler

Vibratory Tumbler Advantages

- Five times faster to a finished product (8 days on average for vibratory vs. 40 days on average for rotary); this not only dramatically increases your production but eliminates the impatience factor for beginners

- Uses 2-3 times less abrasive and polishing compound per load, more than paying for the higher purchase price; this includes the fact that you skip the coarse-grit stage completely

- Less fracturing of stones, which is critical for softer stones and jewelry pendant slabs and cabs

- Top loading allows for inspection of stones and slurry as they process and allows you to add water on the fly

- The top-loading feature makes for easier cleanup; just add soap and water at end of each stage, then empty the tumbler barrel into a bucket

HELPFUL TIP: If you decide to go with one of each tumbler, you should get a large rotary tumbler and a small vibratory tumbler. The small vibratory tumbler will keep up with the larger rotary tumbler. In a two-machine setup, most people will do their initial or "rough" tumbling in the rotary tumbler to shape or round out the stones, and then do the polishing steps in the vibratory tumbler.

Setup and Operation

Rotary Tumblers

The rotary tumbling process is low-maintenance, and you can attain a good skill level quickly. Before getting started you need to decide on where you will be placing the machine. Rotary tumblers operate very quietly, so any enclosed room out of high-traffic areas is a good choice. In the summer you can set them up in a garage or outdoor shed, as long as there is available electric power. In colder climates you'll need to bring your machine indoors when the temperature falls below freezing, or else the water will freeze and halt the tumbling process. A utility room or basement area with concrete flooring is your best bet. We also like to place an old towel (folded over) underneath the machine to absorb any possible leakage (though this is unusual) and to further dampen the sound. As a further precaution against leakage, set the machine in a shallow plastic tray.

Vibratory Tumblers

The vibratory tumbling process will at first seem to be higher maintenance than rotary tumbling. This is primarily due to the short cycles between tumbling stages and the need to periodically check the "moisture factor" inside the barrel. However, it truly is not much more work than rotary tumbling once you get the rhythm of the stages, and you can always slow things down by pouring a cup of water in the barrel and just letting it run; no harm will be done to the stones—they just get a bonus cleaning until you are ready to move them to the next stage.

Since vibratory tumblers make a bit more noise than rotary tumblers, you should put them in an out-of-the-way place and set the tumbler base on an old, double- or triple-folded towel to dampen the vibrations. You should also set the machine in a shallow plastic tray to contain any leakage. You should never cover the tumbler with any type of box (to dampen sound), as the motor will then overheat and potentially break down. And finally, vibratory tumblers (and the plastic tray they are sitting in) should always be placed on a concrete floor when that's an option, to limit the shaking of floors and walls. Some people choose to only run their vibratory tumblers during daytime hours if they don't have a dedicated area for their tumbler.

Tumbling Supplies

Before diving into the instructions for using your tumbler, you need to know about the materials that you'll be using. The tumble polishing process first uses abrasives to smooth the stones and then uses a polishing compound to bring them to a glossy shine (unless you choose a satin finish—see Tumbling and Polish Options, page 53). In addition to abrasives and polishes, you will also need tumbling media or filler stones or pellets to help carry the abrasives and buffer the collisions between gemstones during the tumbling process. The materials we describe below are the same for both rotary and vibratory tumblers; they are just used in varying amounts. All of these materials are commonly available at local and online lapidary supply stores and are generally sold by the pound.

The lapidary supplies you'll need are shown below, and the list is organized in the sequence that they will be used. The abrasives (grits) available from lapidary suppliers are highly uniform, but the polishes can be somewhat specialized. It is highly recommended that you find the type of polishing compound that we show, as it greatly improves your chances of obtaining a high-gloss shine.

Coarse Abrasive (60–80 mesh)
Silicon carbide granules that are large enough to cause substantial removal of rough edges on hard gemstone materials and round out the overall shape of the stone

Medium Abrasive (180–220 mesh)
Silicon carbide granules that remove some rough edges but primarily smooth out the surfaces of gemstones, removing scratches, or grooves from cutting

Fine Abrasive (500 mesh)
Silicon carbide granules in a fine powder that remove minute scratches and prepare the gemstones for polishing

Ultra-fine Abrasive (800 mesh)
Aluminum oxide powder that gives gemstones a final smoothing or sanding effect; most gemstones and product types don't require this stage

Polishing Compound
An aluminum oxide compound that polishes the gemstones, resulting in either a soft glow or a high polish

Tumbling Media

Marble- to pea-size ceramic pellets or gemstone pebbles that are layered in with the gemstones being tumbled; make sure they are the same type and hardness as the stones you are tumbling; best of all, these can be cleaned and reused many times!

Additional Equipment and Supplies
These accessories are a must to make you more efficient, and you probably have most of them already! You just need to set up some space in your lapidary storage and work area to keep them organized and handy for use during the tumbling process.

Two 5-gallon buckets, one for emptying your tumbler barrel between stages, and one for rinsing the gemstones

Liquid hand soap to add during each tumbling stage, and for your super-clean tumbling stage

A large plastic colander to catch your stones as you drain the tumbling barrel

A small scrub brush to wash grit off of the stones between tumbling stages

Seven medium-size plastic containers with locking lids to hold your tumbling grits, polishing compound and tumbling media

 A stack of small plastic shot cups or plastic measuring cups for measuring grit and polishing compound

 A shallow plastic tray to set the tumbler and towel into, in case of leaks

 A spray bottle for increasing the moisture level in vibratory tumblers

 One or two medium-size multi-tray stacking tray units to sort your gemstones between tumbling stages

Getting the Best Tumbling Results

Tumble polishing is an astonishingly simple concept. It consists of just a few tumbling stages (coarse grind, medium grind, fine grind, polishing) and some simple tumbling steps (cleaning the stones, loading the tumbler barrel, running the tumbler). Despite its simplicity, tumble polishing can be frustrating for beginners, especially when tumbled stones come out with loads of chips and fractures, or with a dull luster, even though you followed the instructions you received when you purchased your tumbler. If you follow our simple approach and the corresponding tips and checklists we provide, you can bypass all of the frustration and wasted time and materials.

Tumble polishing is the subject of several complete books, so why do we think we can cover it in a chapter? Experience. We've honed our skills over years of practice, and we've gleaned the essential information you need to help you master tumble polishing and make your work more efficient. What's more, we've developed charts and checklists to accelerate your learning and help you produce beautifully polished gemstones and jewelry pieces! Best of all, on pages 63–65 we provide the Comprehensive Tumbling Chart, an easy-to-reference guide that you'll refer to over and over again. It might be something you want to photocopy and then laminate to keep handy near your tumbling supplies!

Tumbling and Polish Options

While gemstones with high-gloss polish are perennially popular with gemstone enthusiasts, stones with a satin, or semi-gloss, finish are becoming as popular as highly polished gemstones—or even more so. This is true both for stones that will simply be tumbled (or whole agate nodules cut in half first) and set out for display, and for stones that will be used to make jewelry pieces.

The Advantages of a Satin Finish

- It's much faster

- You will use far less abrasive grit and no polishing compound, so the cost is lower

- The tumbling process is much simpler; attention to detail in cleaning is less critical

- Your "housekeeping efforts" between tumbling stages are dramatically reduced; in fact, to achieve a satin finish using a rotary tumbler, we suggest a two-step process consisting of an extended coarse grind and a fine grind—this omits at least one entire tumbling stage, making things even easier

- A satin finish also produces fine-looking specimens, and imperfections are easy to fix; we recommend applying a light coating of mineral oil or good-quality paste wax to stones with slight fractures, to help mask them

Tumbling Stages

With both rotary and vibratory tumblers, you progress through multiple stages before you arrive at a finished product. These stages gradually transform a gemstone's rough and sometimes jagged edges, and each stage produces smoother and smoother surfaces before finally resulting in a high-gloss shine. The Comprehensive Tumbling Chart (pages 63-65) will guide you as to which stages are required, based on the type of finish you desire (satin or polished) and the type of tumbler you are using (vibratory or rotary).

before tumbling

The Coarse Grind Stage removes sharp and angular surfaces, providing smooth and rounded stones.
(**Note:** This stage is not performed with vibratory tumblers, as the coarse grit can damage a vibratory tumbler's barrel!)

after coarse grinding

The Medium Grind Stage smooths and sands the stones and provides a bit more rounding.

after medium grinding

The Fine Grind Stage creates a satin (semi-gloss) finish but does not do any additional rounding or shaping.

The Super-Clean Stage removes any remaining abrasive grit that may be hiding in small cracks or pits in the stones.

after fine grinding

HELPFUL TIP: For rotary tumblers, you should be cautious when using soap, as it may result in pressure buildup within the tumbler barrel; if you use soap for your super-clean stage, make sure to limit the run time to one hour or less.

The Pre-Polish Stage is used infrequently and only for the highest-grade stones to get the maximum polish and shine; this does not do any additional rounding or shaping. Rotary tumblers don't require this stage.

The Polishing Stage applies polishing compounds that bind to the gemstones, resulting in a high-gloss shine.

after polishing

HELPFUL TIP: With rotary tumblers, it's possible to consolidate the coarse and medium grind stages. This requires less cleanup and uses less polishing abrasive. You will achieve nearly the same quality of polished stones by simply running the rotary tumbler for the combined amount of time of the two stages (for example, 8 days for the coarse grind stage + 8 days for the medium grind stage = 16 total days of running time).

Tumbling Process Steps

The tumbling process involves a series of steps that you repeat as you proceed through each tumbling stage. The steps are as follows:

1) Load the tumbling barrel.

2) Add abrasive tumbling grit or polishing compound, and if you have a vibratory tumbler, add two pumps of liquid hand soap.

3) Run the tumbler for the prescribed time period.

4) Empty and clean the tumbling barrel and stones.

The illustration below reflects the relationship between tumbling steps and stages. Each stage progresses through the same steps, starting with loading the tumbler barrel.

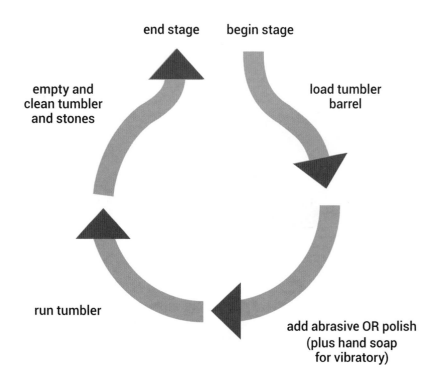

Getting Started

Step 1: Load the Tumbler Barrel

When loading your tumbler barrel you must use stones (and tumbling media) of the same hardness. This ensures that the harder stones don't fracture or crush the softer stones.

HELPFUL TIP: Before you start dropping the stones into the tumbler barrel, fill the barrel ¼–⅓ full of water. Putting water into the barrel first helps prevent ugly fractures or blemishes.

When you load a tumbling barrel, it must be balanced; specifically, you need to use a mixture of sizes of gemstones and tumbling media within the tumbling barrel. The easiest way to do this is to place stones in layers. Start with small stones and tumbling media, then medium-size stones (or jewelry pieces), and then larger stones. Then, repeat the sequence until the barrel is about 75 percent full, finishing with a layer of small stones and tumbling media.

empty space

small stones & tumbling media

larger stones

medium stones & jewelry slabs

small stones & tumbling media

larger stones

medium stones & jewelry slabs

small stones & tumbling media

Once you have completed loading the barrel (to 75 percent full), add or pour out water as necessary to obtain the proper water level for each tumbler type, as described below.

Rotary Tumblers

The water level should be just below the top layer of stones, which means you should be able to see the water level beneath the top layer, but it should not cover the top layer of stones. Leaving some space allows you to use your kitchen sprayer or a spray bottle to remove any abrasive that is in the top rim of the tumbling barrel. This prevents cracking and chipping.

loaded rotary tumbler barrel

Vibratory Tumblers

Drain the water from the tumbler, leaving the stones dripping wet. Too much water will not allow the tumbling abrasives to bond effectively with the stones and perform the necessary grinding and smoothing. We also recommend that you add two pumps of liquid hand soap, as it will improve the adhesion of the abrasive grit to the stones during tumbling.

For larger barrels (such as the 12-lb.), you might be able to fit three or four sets of layers; with the smaller barrels (such as the 3-lb.), you might only get one or two sets of layers, and the stones you'll be able to fit in the tumbler will be considerably smaller.

Step 2: Add the Abrasive or Polish

On pages 63–65 of this chapter, you'll find the Comprehensive Tumbling Chart. Photocopy it, laminate it and keep it handy near your work area, as it will show you how much abrasive or polishing compound is needed for each tumbling stage and for each type and size of tumbler. (**Note:** Always add the abrasive grit or polishing compound after you have adjusted the water level in the tumbling barrel; this is literally the last thing you will do before closing the lid tightly and starting your tumbling run.)

HELPFUL TIP: Many lapidary pros suggest adding one pump of liquid hand soap as a means of improving the binding of abrasive grit to the gemstones. Use caution when doing this with a rotary tumbler, as soap may result in a pressure buildup inside the tumbling barrel. Some people have even had the unpleasant experience of the lid blowing off the tumbler, making a big mess. This is another good reason to place your tumbler on top of an old towel set in a shallow plastic tray.

Step 3: Run the Tumbler

Now it's time to actually run the tumbler. To determine how long you need to run it, refer to the Comprehensive Tumbling Chart. This will show you the recommended run times for each type of tumbler and tumbling stage. You can generally run the tumbler for a bit longer than our recommendations (like an extra couple of days with rotary tumblers, or a few extra hours with vibratory tumblers), but if you run for much longer than this, you're only adding to the wear on your tumbler and increasing the risk of fracturing your gemstones. Some older books on tumbling insist that you need to periodically open your tumbler to inspect the stones or release trapped gases that may build up inside the tumbler barrel. Our recommendation for rotary tumblers is to just let them run. You can periodically check to ensure it isn't leaking and that you can hear the stones gently rolling in the tumbler. (**Note:** Don't let your tumbler sit for any length of time without running. The contents will settle to the bottom of the barrel and harden like concrete.)

Special Considerations for Vibratory Tumblers

Top loading. One major benefit of vibratory tumblers is that they are top loading, which means that they sit vertically rather than horizontally while they are running. Additionally, the lid is generally not screwed on, so you can quickly open and close it while the machine is running. This not only makes the process of adjusting the moisture level very quick and easy, it also allows you to conduct "rapid rinses" when you're moving between stages.

Adjusting the "moisture factor." Since vibratory tumblers don't have standing water, you need to periodically check to see that the slurry (water and tumbling abrasive or polishing compound) is

too dry   correct moisture

maintaining a semi-liquid consistency. If the slurry begins to appear dry or pasty, simply spray a couple squirts from a spray bottle into the barrel and put the lid back on. Usually this only needs to be done once or twice during a 12- to 24-hour tumbling stage.

Multiple Runs of Stages 2-6. If you want that ultimate high-gloss shine with very high-grade pieces, the medium grind, fine grind, super-clean, pre-polish and polish stages can each be run twice in a row. But with that said, you still get a beautiful shine with a single run of each tumbling stage, so this is truly optional.

Rapid Rinsing. At the completion of each tumbling stage, you'll find your cleanup goes a lot faster by doing a "rapid rinse" inside the tumbler. While the tumbler is still running, add one or two squirts of liquid soap and ½ cup of water, put the lid back on and let the tumbler run for 10 minutes. Then open and add enough water to cover the stones and let the tumbler run for 10 more minutes. Turn off the tumbler and drain into your 5-gallon bucket, or on the ground outside, by using a colander to catch your stones and tumbling media.

Step 4: Empty and Clean the Tumbler Barrel and Stones

Every experienced lapidary hobbyist will tell you that cleaning is the most important step in producing high-quality polished gemstones. If you take a little extra time to thoroughly clean your gemstones and the tumbling barrel between tumbling stages, you'll save countless wasted hours and save on tumbling materials. When we say thorough, we mean thorough—you need to remove all of the tumbling grit and any broken, chipped and deeply pitted or fractured stones present. This prevents them from scratching the surfaces of your gemstones during subsequent tumbling stages. The exception to this rule is the coarse grind stage, which will often start with stones that have rough and broken surfaces.

To clean your gemstones, follow the steps below:

1) Place your plastic colander atop a 5-gallon bucket. Open the tumbler and gently pour out the contents of the tumbler barrel into the colander. Use a kitchen sprayer or garden hose sprayer to rinse the grit off of the stones and into the bucket below.

2) Fill a second 5-gallon pail (or washroom bucket) about half full with water and gently place your gemstones and tumbling media into the bucket. If you are moving between tumbling stages, you will be emptying the stones from your plastic colander into

the bucket. Keep the stones immersed in water to reduce drying and potential additional fracturing. Massage the stones with your hands and scrub any stones that have small pits, to remove sand, dirt and particles of tumbling abrasive.

3) Clean the tumbling barrel with a small scrub brush and/or heavy-duty paper towels to remove any abrasive from the corners and seams within the tumbling barrel. You want your tumbler barrel to be squeaky clean before moving to the next tumbling cycle. Fill the tumbler barrel $^{1}/_{3}$ –$^{1}/_{2}$ full with water.

4) As you get the stones cleaned and scrubbed, you can start placing them back into the clean tumbler barrel for the next stage. When you do so, be sure to remove any cracked, broken or deeply pitted stones, and either discard them or put them back into your rough rock bin.

5) Empty the buckets outside, not down an interior sink or drain! Even small amounts of leftover tumbling abrasives or dirt and sand will eventually clog and close off your interior plumbing, resulting in an expensive repair.

6) You are now ready to move to the next stage.

HELPFUL TIPS:

1. The most important step of the cleaning process is to remove all of the tumbling grit and any broken, chipped and any deeply pitted or fractured gemstones, so that they don't scratch the surfaces of your gemstones.

2. Even though gemstones are very hard, you need to keep them wet and handle them gently between tumbling stages. Many beautiful stones have been ruined by rough handling between stages.

3. Abrasive grit will settle at the bottom of the 5-gallon bucket that you first empty your tumbler into. Some people try to reuse the tumbling grit, but this is neither cost effective nor reliable. It's better to just discard this material.

Comprehensive Tumbling Chart

Because rotary and vibratory machines are different and gemstones vary in hardness, the number of stages necessary to reach a finished product can vary significantly. That's why we've included the Comprehensive Tumbling Chart, on pages 64-65. It's not an exaggeration to say that this tumbling chart will be your lifelong friend. Photocopy it, laminate it and hang it up by your tumbling workstation. The chart is simple to use—select a few variables (such as tumbler type and size, which tumbling stage you are on, and whether you want a satin or high-gloss finish) and it tells you exactly how long to tumble your gemstones, plus type and quantity of abrasive or polishing compound to use.

We are only providing you with the details for the three tumblers that are featured in this book. Nonetheless, if you have a larger tumbler, it's not difficult to calculate how much abrasive and polish you'll need. As a general rule of thumb, you can just scale up the amounts listed on the chart. So if our chart shows a 4-lb. vibratory tumbler but you have a 10-lb. vibratory tumbler, then simply multiply by 2.5 to get the correct amount of grit and polish for each cycle. (The run time will remain the same.) To keep things simple, after multiplying you can round up to the next whole number, as a larger machine often means a bit more abrasive or grit will be needed.

Comprehensive Tumbling Chart
(photocopy for display in your workshop)

TYPE OF STONE	FINISH TYPE	#1: COARSE (60–80 MESH)	#2: MEDIUM (180–220 MESH)	#3: SANDING/FINE (500 MESH)
3-lb. Rotary Tumbler				
Agate, Jasper, Quartz, Tiger Eye, Petrified Wood, Obsidian	polish	4 Tbsp, 8 days	4 Tbsp, 8 days	6 Tbsp, 10 days
Apache Tears, Turquoise	polish	4 Tbsp, 6 days	4 Tbsp, 6 days	6 Tbsp, 8 days
Agate, Jasper, Quartz, Tiger Eye, Petrified Wood, Obsidian	satin	4 Tbsp, 15 days	skip	6 Tbsp, 10 days
Apache Tears, Turquoise	satin	4 Tbsp, 12 days	skip	6 Tbsp, 8 days
12-lb. Rotary Tumbler				
Agate, Jasper, Quartz, Tiger Eye, Petrified Wood, Obsidian	polish	20 Tbsp, 8 days	20 Tbsp, 8 days	24 Tbsp, 10 days
Apache Tears, Turquoise	polish	20 Tbsp, 6 days	20 Tbsp, 6 days	24 Tbsp, 8 days
Agate, Jasper, Quartz, Tiger Eye, Petrified Wood, Obsidian	satin	20 Tbsp, 15 days	skip	24 Tbsp, 10 days
Apache Tears, Turquoise	satin	20 Tbsp, 12 days	skip	24 Tbsp, 8 days
4.5-lb. Vibratory Tumbler				
Agate, Jasper, Quartz, Tiger Eye, Petrified Wood, Obsidian	polish	skip	Run 1: 2 Tbsp, 24 hr *Run 2: 1 Tbsp, 12 hr	Run 1: 1 Tbsp, 24 hr *Run 2: ½ Tbsp, 12 hr
Apache Tears, Turquoise	polish	skip	Run 1: 2 Tbsp, 12 hr *Run 2: 1 Tbsp, 12 hr	Run 1: 1 Tbsp, 12 hr *Run 2: ½ Tbsp, 12 hr
Agate, Jasper, Quartz, Tiger Eye, Petrified Wood, Obsidian	satin	skip	Run 1: 2 Tbsp, 24 hr *Run 2: 1 Tbsp, 12 hr	Run 1: 1 Tbsp, 24 hr *Run 2: ½ Tbsp, 12 hr
Apache Tears, Turquoise	satin	skip	Run 1: 2 Tbsp, 12 hr *Run 2: 1 Tbsp, 12 hr	Run 1: 1 Tbsp, 12 hr *Run 2: ½ Tbsp, 12 hr

* Optional, for the highest-quality results; see page 60

#4: SUPER-CLEAN (LIQUID SOAP)	#5: PRE-POLISH (800 MESH)	#6: POLISH (ALUMINUM OXIDE)	TOTAL TIME	TOTAL GRIT/POLISH
1 pump (1 hour max!)	skip	6 Tbsp, 7 days	33 days	20 Tbsp
1 pump (1 hour max!)	skip	6 Tbsp, 7 days	27 days	20 Tbsp
1 pump (1 hour max!)	skip	skip	25 days	10 Tbsp
1 pump (1 hour max!)	skip	skip	20 days	10 Tbsp
1 pump (1 hour max!)	skip	24 Tbsp, 7 days	33 days	88 Tbsp
1 pump (1 hour max!)	skip	24 Tbsp, 7 days	27 days	88 Tbsp
1 pump (1 hour max!)	skip	skip	25 days	44 Tbsp
1 pump (1 hour max!)	skip	skip	20 days	44 Tbsp
Run 1: 1 pump, 1 hr *Run 2: 1 pump, 1 hr	(optional stage) Run 1: 1 tsp, 12 hr *Run 2: 1 tsp, 12 hr	Run 1: 1 tsp, 12 hr *Run 2: 1 tsp, 12 hr	5–7 days	6 Tbsp
Run 1: 1 pump, 1 hr *Run 2: 1 pump, 1 hr	(optional stage) Run 1: 1 tsp, 12 hr *Run 2: 1 tsp, 12 hr	Run 1: 1 tsp, 12 hr *Run 2: 1 tsp, 12 hr	5–6 days	6 Tbsp
Run 1: 1 pump, 1 hr *Run 2: 1 pump, 1 hr	skip	skip	3 days	5 Tbsp
Run 1: 1 pump, 1 hr *Run 2: 1 pump, 1 hr	skip	skip	2 days	5 Tbsp

* Optional, for the highest-quality results; see page 60

Equipment

- Buying a good-quality tumbler is well worth the investment. Inexpensive tumblers will wear out quickly, produce poor results and make excessive noise; they just might cause you to quit altogether.

Stone Selection and Preparation Work

- Garbage in = shiny garbage out. Don't expect to turn low-grade flower-planter stones into jewelry-grade stones simply by tumble polishing them.

- Many stones need to be cut to expose their most beautiful patterns or features.

Supplies

- For each tumbling abrasive or polish, use a separate plastic measuring cup. These are very cheap; buy a stack of 2-oz. measuring cups for a couple dollars and you'll be set for life.

- Ceramic tumbling media or a variety of low-quality stones of the same type you are tumbling are superior to plastic pellets, which tend to float and then bunch together, rather than remain evenly distributed.

- Only use the high-grade, aluminum oxide polish specified in this book; buying cheaper materials causes you to perform additional polishing or burnishing stages, resulting in long times and higher costs for extra polishing compound.

Setup

- Place your tumbler in an area away from high-traffic and noise-sensitive areas.

- Place an old towel or a piece of old carpet underneath the tumbler to catch any leakage and dampen the vibrations and noise; place these in a shallow plastic tray to further reduce the chance of any leakage.

- Keep your abrasives and polishes in a cool, dry place and inside of tightly closed containers (inexpensive plastic containers with locking lids or zip-top bags are fine).

- Keep a checklist or log sheet of your tumbling activities and your own personal tips and tricks; this is especially valuable when you are getting started.

- "Life-cycling" is a great way to enjoy your tumbling activity; in other words, plan your tumbling schedule around your free times so you don't feel rushed.

Processing

- Never empty a tumbler barrel down the drain; the abrasive grit will turn into a concrete-like mixture, settle in your drain traps, harden and close off the openings. This can result in a very expensive plumbing repair project!

- In summer, "dirty rinse" outdoors with a hose and a colander; in winter, "dirty rinse" indoors with a colander and 5-gallon bucket (eventually the bucket will need to be emptied outdoors).

- Clean your stones thoroughly between stages; put them in a bucket of water (to keep them wet between stages) and scrub them with a small brush. Pay extra attention to stones with deep pits where abrasives can get trapped (you might choose to discard these). Do a cleansing run before the fine grind stage and the polishing stage—just soap and water for an hour or two in a vibratory tumbler, and with water only (no soap) for 12-24 hours in a rotary tumbler.

- Clean your tumbler barrel and lid thoroughly between stages. A spray bottle is great for getting grit out of the inner ring of your tumbler barrel, where the lid rests. Using a paper towel to rub out the inside after the barrel has been rinsed is also a good idea.

- Handle rocks with care to avoid cracking and chipping; partially fill your tumbler barrel with water first ($1/4$–$1/3$ full), then carefully place stones into the barrel (adjust the amount of water to the proper level after filling). When removing stones, pour the stones out slowly, and only use a gentle shaking motion to remove them if you cannot get your hand into the tumbler barrel; a plastic spoon or spatula can also be used to scoop out stones.

- Don't mix stones of different hardness in the same barrel; the softer stones will break.

- Mix the sizes of stones within a single batch to maximize the tumbling and grinding/sanding/polishing action.

- If you are tumbling jewelry pendant slabs or cabochons, layer small stones or tumbling media in between each layer of slabs/cabs; usually a ratio of 60 percent tumbling media to 40 percent slabs/cabs will give good results (75 percent tumbling media is even better; use this for your very best stones).

- Between stages, remove any stones that are broken or have rough or sharp edges.

- After loading your vibratory tumbler barrel and putting in your tumbling abrasive or polish, add two pumps of liquid hand soap, to help the abrasive stick to the stones better and to improve cleaning.

- Don't over-tend your tumbler, especially rotary tumblers—turning the tumbler off and on can cause the grit to settle in a clump at the bottom of the tumbler. Some old books on tumbling say you will get gas build-up and possibly even explosions if you don't periodically open the lid of your tumbler; this is exceedingly rare and thus not necessary.

- For rotary tumblers, you can do a two-stage process for a satin finish and a three-stage process for polishing by running the coarse grit for 10-25 days. This saves on grit, cleaning time and overall effort. Make sure to keep the tumbler running to ensure the grit doesn't solidify in the barrel; in general don't turn off the tumbler until just before emptying it.

- For most hobbyists, detailed inspection of the stones with a magnifying lens between tumbling stages is unnecessary. You can feel and see broken, cracked and deeply pitted stones with your unaided eyes and your bare hands. The same goes for determining if your gemstones are smooth enough; if you follow our instructions, you should be fine.

- Running rotary tumblers for excessive amounts of time leads to more fracturing, so follow our recommendations in the Comprehensive Tumbling Chart on pages 63-65. With that said, it is okay to run an extra day or two for rotary tumblers or a few extra hours with vibratory machines.

Cutting

What It Is

One use for a lapidary saw is slabbing, which means cutting your gemstones into slabs or slices, the first step in making many lapidary products, including necklace pendants. Lapidary saws are also used for cutting gemstone slabs into shapes (referred to as cabochons) or for rough cutting (removing rough or uneven sections from gemstones), which is often necessary before polishing a gemstone. In addition, rough cutting is useful if you have a whole gemstone you want to slice open (such as a whole agate nodule) and subsequently polish.

Process Overview

Cutting gemstones involves gemstone selection, starting the cut, rocking and rolling (which help make a clean cut and avoid damage to the saw blade), and cleaning up any rough areas from the cut. After a cut is complete, stones must then be cleaned before they can be used in lapidary projects such as dome polishing or cabochon making.

Equipment and Lapidary Supplies

Gemstone slabbing and cutting require a lapidary saw. Lapidary saws use either an oil-based or a water-based lubricant (which also acts as a coolant and helps to flush away debris) and can cut through very hard gemstone materials. We strongly recommend using diamond-coated, sintered-rim saw blades to obtain clean cuts and make the best use of your precious gemstones.

Process Highlights

Gemstone selection and careful use of the saw are the keys to successful gemstone cutting. By following our specific tips, including rocking and rolling a stone while cutting (see page 82), you're more likely to have success.

Time Requirements

It doesn't take long to make a cut through a stone, just 30-60 seconds for smaller stones and up to 3 minutes for larger gemstones with a higher hardness rating (such as agates). If you will be cutting several slabs out of a single stone, simply multiply the time needed to make one cut by the number of cuts you need to make.

Recommended Equipment

There are technically two kinds of rock saws for cutting slabs—
slab saws and trim saws—and you can use either to cut small- to
medium-size gemstone materials. For amateur hobbyists, we
strongly recommend that it's only necessary to purchase a
good-quality trim saw, since it can be used both for cutting slabs
and for trim cutting, which is part of the cabochon making process.
And while we generally only recommend one model of equipment
in this book, in this case we include two, because they operate with
different lubricants, and each offers its own advantages and
drawbacks. (In addition to the saws shown below, other quality
saw brands are Covington Engineering, Diamond Pacific and
Barranca Diamond.)

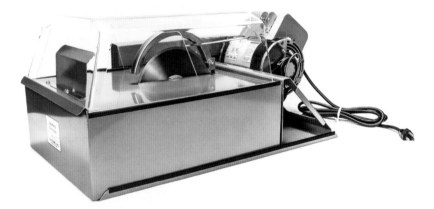

The Lortone 8" Trim Saw

The Lortone 8" trim saw uses rockhound oil, which is non-toxic
but can make something of a mess, and you need to purchase more
rockhound oil from time to time. The oil is relatively inexpensive,
so the cleanup factor is probably the bigger issue; thankfully, if you
take the proper precautions (see page 74), you can prevent much of
the mess.

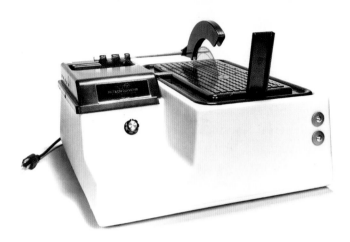

The High-Tech Diamond 6" Trim Saw

The High-Tech Diamond 6" trim saw uses water as a lubricant. While you still need to control the spray in order to avoid a mess, it is certainly cheaper than an oil-cooled saw, and you don't have to contend with an oily spray or mist that can't be completely controlled.

Setup and Operation

Noise is a major consideration when operating a rock saw. Operating your saw in a remote basement, garage or shed is a great way to help you keep peace with your family (or the neighbors in an adjoining condo).

Cleanliness is also an issue, since there will always be some fine mist or spray escaping into the air around the saw. You will probably want to hang a cheap plastic tarp behind your saw, and you'll also want to cover the floor in your work area and cover any nearby items you want to keep completely free of mist. This is especially important if your saw uses oil-based lubricants.

Other Places to Saw

The saws we recommend are portable, so if there are other areas where you can set up and operate your saw, you can do so. Examples include a shop area at a local school, a community center, or even your place of employment. The best option of all is to find a local gem and mineral club that has a space rental or usage agreement at a local community center, school or so on. Because lapidary work is quite diverse, such venues are a great place to learn some new tricks or about different kinds of lapidary creations. And different people have different machines, so you might not have to purchase all of the equipment on your own!

Safety

You might be wondering about the safety of lapidary trim saws. Surprisingly, the diamond saw blades they use rarely break the surface of your skin, so you won't need to wear any protective gloves. But we do recommend a few safety measures, such as wearing wrap-around protective eyewear and

using headphones (or earplugs) to dampen the sound. As long as you take precautions and wear protective eyewear, cutting gemstone slabs is safe and relatively easy when you have the right equipment and supplies.

Note: There is a serious health condition known as silicosis that results from breathing in excessive amounts of rock dust. Use of lubricants when cutting and grinding is the most important way to minimize chances of developing this condition. We also strongly recommend having a good ventilating fan. As an additional precaution, you can use a respirator or mask to further reduce the possibility of breathing in rock dust.

Saw Blades

While your choice of saw is important, your choice of saw blade is even more important. Rock saws are able to cut through rock because they are coated with materials that are even harder than the gemstones they cut. There are two different types of blade coatings: silicon carbide and pulverized diamonds. Silicon carbide is the same material as rock tumbling grit. Saw blades with a silicon carbide coating were once popular, but thanks to improvements in materials technology, blades coated with pulverized diamonds are now much more popular.

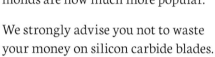

We strongly advise you not to waste your money on silicon carbide blades. While they are cheaper, you get what you pay for. A diamond blade will last much longer and will cut much faster. In addition, diamond-coated blades make cleaner cuts than silicon carbide ones; this helps protect your precious gemstones from additional chips, fractures or deeply cut grooves.

About Diamond Blades

As you might expect, manufacturing diamond-covered blades is somewhat complicated. In a process called sintering, crushed diamonds are applied to specialized metals. This results in a narrow strip or rim of diamond coating around the edge of the saw blade. When the blade is used, this edge gradually wears away. When the gold-colored sintered portion is gone, you need to purchase a new blade.

HELPFUL TIP: To get the maximum life out of your diamond saw blades, we strongly recommend purchasing an inexpensive saw blade dressing stick. Periodically make a couple of thin cuts through the dressing stick. To make things simple, do this every time you are done using the saw for the day.

Recommended Blade Thickness

Diamond saw blades differ in thickness. We recommend buying a .032" blade; this blade is of a medium thickness and is suitable for cutting the gemstones in this book. Thinner blades do have their advantages—a thinner blade wastes less gemstone material and can give a more precise cut, but these blades are more subject to warping and hence more sensitive in their use.

Lubricants

If your rock saw requires an oil-based lubricant, it will almost always be best to use a product known as lapidary or rockhound oil, which is available from all lapidary supply companies. This mineral-based oil is neutral in terms of odor and features excellent cooling properties that extend the life of your saw blade and your saw.

Additional Equipment and Supplies

These accessories are a must to make you more efficient, and you probably have most of them already. If not, you'll see they are quite economical! You just need to set up some space in your lapidary work area to keep things handy while you're actually cutting rock.

 Sound-blocking headphones or earplugs

 Protective eyewear, such as goggles or safety glasses

 A hat or baseball cap to keep oil or water spray off of your hair

 Plastic trays for sorting and storing materials at the cutting station

 Buckets and other storage containers; plastic ice cream buckets or potato/macaroni salad pails are perfect for storing your gemstone materials waiting to be cut

Disposable painter's masks

A painting tarp to protect your walls from oil and water spray

Shop rags for cleanup, the cheaper the better; old socks work great, too

Optional: an improvised plastic or cardboard shield, if your saw doesn't have one built in

Making the Best Cut

First, you need to decide what you'll be creating. Are you simply cutting a whole agate nodule in half, or are you cutting away the rough surface of a stone and then face polishing the cut surfaces? Or perhaps you are creating jewelry slabs or slices.

If you're creating jewelry, there are two different ways to use your saw. You can either create whole-stone, natural-form slabs or rough slabs that will be further cut and shaped. Agates are commonly cut into natural-form slabs, and while you have the option of trimming whole-stone agate slabs to symmetrical shapes (ovals, for example), many people prefer to leave them in a natural shape or a form that follows the shape of the stone. Petrified wood and jasper are two materials that are commonly cut into rough slabs and then further cut into symmetrical shapes. Unlike agates, these gemstone materials tend to come in large chunks or blocks, so they don't lend to making small, natural-shape jewelry pendants.

Once you have decided on what you want to create, you need to figure out how to get the best possible rock slabs or face cuts from your gemstones. This aspect of gemstone cutting is highly intuitive, which means there is no perfect way to decide how and where to cut into your materials, and you will develop your own techniques as you spend more time with your favorite types of gemstones.

Of course, the best way to learn is simple: practice. We strongly recommend practicing on lower-quality materials and specimens before you start

Below-grade Montana moss agates

cutting higher-grade gemstones. This will get you comfortable with using the saw, and it's a great way to practice other important parts of the sawing process.

Lapidary-grade Montana moss agate slices

Prior to making any cuts, there are a number of important factors to consider before actually turning on the saw. The following general guidelines will help determine how to cut, your cutting angle and the width of your cuts.

Don't Waste Material

Before you cut, estimate how many slabs or slices can be obtained from the stone. If you're cutting multiple slices, consider how thick they need to be for your planned use (in jewelry, etc.).

Highlight the Most Attractive Features

Cut at an angle that exposes the most striking features. Sometimes you will need to make an "exploratory cut" near the outer surface on one side of the stone; this can help you determine subsequent cuts that will yield the best slabs that highlight natural colors and patterns.

Remove Flawed Areas

Always remove the rough and fractured sections of stone first, but remove the smallest amount of stone possible; if you discover additional fracturing after the first cut, the stone is probably better suited for tumbling filler or use as a display stone in an aquarium.

Square Up the Sides

Depending on the thickness of the stone, you might need to cut away the rough exterior surfaces on both sides first in order to get multiple interior slabs with flat surfaces.

Starting a Cut

When cutting away the rough exterior surface, start your cut from the side of the stone where you will be cutting away the most material; this helps the saw blade get a solid entry and "bite" into the stone. This will also create a smoother and more even surface and will make sanding and polishing your gemstones easier later.

For a Slab to Drill Through

If you're planning on drilling through a slab (called face drilling) to make a jewelry piece, thin slabs are best. Drilling through thick cuts is costly (drill bits are expensive) and time consuming; if you're planning on using a piece for jewelry, we specifically recommend a maximum thickness of $^1/_8$–$^1/_4$".

Cutting a Whole Stone

Cutting whole stones is tricky, especially if there are no visible features, such as patterns, on the outside to guide you. If there is no visible pattern, cut the stone across its widest point. This will give you the largest possible slabs, if that's how you intend to cut it; it also will expose the maximum amount of surface area if you are polishing the face of each half. If there is exposed pattern (as often happens with agates), you should cut at an angle that highlights the pattern.

Avoid Cutting Very Large Stones

If your stone is substantially thicker than the height of the saw blade above the table (which is 2" for a 6" saw blade and 3" for an 8" saw blade), you will have to roll the stone 180 degrees to be able to fully cut through it. Stones that require this might be too large for the saw; cutting them can result in uneven wear on your diamond saw blade—and it could even bend the blade, rendering your expensive diamond blade useless!

How to Hold a Gemstone While Cutting

Once you have decided where to cut, it's time to start cutting. Some rock saws have a pre-installed vise and a guide-bar device that can be used to hold your gemstones in place while you push them through the rotating saw blade. While these types of setups can be useful for cutting large pieces of gemstone material or for high-precision, high-volume cutting, they are completely  unnecessary for hobbyists, and we will not address them. Additionally, using such vises and guides makes it more likely that you'll break off chunks of stone at the front or back of the cutting surface, as you can't use the rocking and rolling technique that we'll describe, but instead have to cut straight through from front to back; this is especially problematic when you are cutting natural-shape jewelry slices.

Instead of depending on a piece of equipment or a technological gizmo, the best way to hold a gemstone is much simpler: use your hands. When cutting, you will generally hold the stones between the thumb, forefinger and middle finger of both hands in something of a pincer/claw arrangement. (**Note:** As mentioned above, cutting gemstones is a relatively safe process; that said, always remember to use the protective equipment and follow the safety measures described on page 75—protective eyewear being the most critical.)

Getting Started

Step 1: Starting the Cut

Once you've got a good hold on the stone, guide it straight into the saw blade. When doing so, it's important to avoid exerting any side-to-side pressure, as this bends or tilts the saw blade and will eventually cause the blade to warp. This is also much more likely to cause your gemstone materials to fracture or break as the blade comes through the last portion of the stone.

Step 2: Rock and Roll

After your stone is about halfway through the blade, you should begin to gently roll (rotate) the stone backward and forward as you guide it through the saw blade in three separate stages:

First, roll the front (farthest from you) edge of the stone up toward you slightly. This causes the blade to cut through more of the underside. When you've cut through about 75 percent of the underside, roll the stone back to its original position.

Next, roll the back edge of the stone up and forward, cutting through more of the topside of the stone, until there is only a thin strip of uncut material left between the cuts on the top and bottom of the gemstone.

Now again roll the stone back to its original position and then slowly cut through the remaining material as you rock the stone back and forth very gently. As you're doing so, try to apply only slight pressure against the saw blade, moving the stone forward only gradually. Learning this trick takes practice, but it's important because it makes it far less likely that your gemstones will break or fracture as the blade comes through the last portion of the stone.

Step 3: Clean Up the Cut

When you have cut completely through your stone, you might notice that there is a slight lip or burr on the edge of one or both pieces of the gemstone material. You can gently place the stone against the saw blade near the lip, and rotate the stone slowly to cut away the excess. This material can also be ground off or tumbled away, but it's sometimes best to remove more significant protrusions with the saw.

Step 4: Clean Your Stones

As a final step we recommend thoroughly cleaning your stones before polishing or tumbling them. Ideally, it's best to clean batches of cut stones all at once, as this make your work more efficient. The following steps and cleaning materials should be used:

1) If you're making cabochons, immerse stones in Floor Dry oil absorbent for 24–48 hours.

2) Soak the stones in Simple Green all-purpose cleaner overnight.

3) Wash your stones with a grease-fighting dish detergent in warm water. Gently massage them and then towel dry.

HELPFUL TIP: For the best results with high-quality gemstones, follow all three steps, but for most medium-grade stones, Step 3 is all that's needed.

Remember . . .

- Safety with rock saws is simple: Always wear a good pair of protective glasses, and to help control dust, always use a lubricant when cutting and work in a well-ventilated area. Noise-dampening headphones and a dust mask are the only other things you might need.

- Rocking and rolling your stones gently in three separate stages will result in fewer breaks and fractures and prolong the life of your saw blade.

- Never apply sideways pressure to the gemstone material and saw blade; it will warp the blade and may fracture your gemstones.

- To keep the peace, find an out-of-the-way place to do your rock cutting and consider the hour of day that you enjoy your sawing.

- Don't try to cut stones that are too large for your saw blade, as it tends to cause uneven wear on the expensive diamond blades. As a rule, the stone should not be thicker than the height of the saw blade above the surface of the saw table.

- The importance of using a high-quality sintered diamond blade cannot be overemphasized. While these blades cost in the range of $60, when used properly they will have a very long life and produce hundreds (if not thousands) of cuts. Inexpensive rock saw blades and floor tile blades take three to four times as long to produce cuts (especially for slabs) and result in much more scratching and scarring; these blemishes are difficult to remove with tumbling and grinding.

- To get the maximum life out of your diamond saw blades, we strongly recommend purchasing an inexpensive saw blade dressing stick. Periodically make a couple of thin cuts through the dressing stick. To make things simple, do this every time you are done using the saw, as your last cut of the day!

What It Is

Face polishing is a method for grinding away a stone's rough features on one surface and then smoothing and polishing that surface to a high-gloss shine. A nicely finished stone can then show both the natural rough exterior and a beautifully polished "face." Ideally, this will highlight the most striking colors and patterns available on the gemstone.

Process Overview

Face polishing involves a successive series of grinding, sanding and polishing stages. The process begins with grinding away any rough edges on the face and roughly shaping the surface. (If you are starting with stone that has been cut with a saw, you will create a beveled edge around the cut surface before performing the shaping.) This is followed by sanding away the scratches and grooves left from the grinding process and then further smoothing the surface. The polishing stage is then used to create a polished, glossy surface; this stage can be skipped if a satin (semi-gloss) finish is desired.

Equipment and Lapidary Supplies

Face polishing requires a rotary, flat-disc lapidary sanding machine (often called a flat-lap), diamond-coated grinding and sanding discs, a special polishing disc, polishing paste and diamond extender fluid.

Process Highlights

Patience and careful inspection of your work are the keys to successful face polishing. While it's possible to rush through the polishing process in relatively short order, this often produces poor-quality work.

Time Requirements

One of the primary benefits of face polishing is that you can create beautifully finished gemstones in less than an hour, as opposed to the days or weeks required when using tumblers. Face polishing involves a number of stages, but it is practically possible to finish a stone in far less time than we recommend (some would say 15 minutes). Nonetheless, you will achieve the most pleasing results if you take a bit more time and go step by step, running multiple stones through each stage before proceeding on to the next one. (In the lapidary biz this is referred to as gang running your stones.)

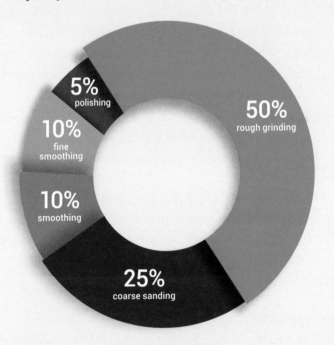

5%
polishing

10%
fine
smoothing

10%
smoothing

50%
rough grinding

25%
coarse sanding

Recommended Equipment

Flat-Disc Lapidary Sanders vs. Vertical Sanders

We strongly recommended using a flat-disc lapidary sanding machine, which is often referred to as a flat-lap. These machines are incredibly easy to use, portable and will stand the test of time; they are also a fraction of the cost of commercial-grade, vertically oriented machines. Flat-disc sanders use diamond-coated grinding discs and produce gemstones and cabochons with a high-gloss polish.

Purchasing a Face Polishing Machine

Face polishing gemstones used to be an expensive process that required large, multi-wheel grinding machines. Today, things are different. Thanks to the prevalence of flat-laps, face polishing is no longer as expensive, noisy or difficult as it once was. We recommend the 8" Ameritool flat lapidary sanding machine, shown above. At about $400, it is a relatively inexpensive machine that is an absolute workhorse. Even if you do eventually purchase a larger vertical-wheel machine, you will still often find yourself using this flat-lap machine, given how quiet and easy to use it is. Other quality flat-disc lapidary sander brands are Hi-Tech Diamond and Crystalite.

Setup and Operation

The flat-lap variety of face polishing machine makes little or no mess. With that said, if you also have a lapidary saw, it's probably a good idea to set up your face polishing workstation in the same area. In addition, as you go through the sequential grinding, sanding and polishing stages, you'll be inspecting your gemstones often, so your work area should be well lit.

Flat-Disc Lapidary Sander Supplies

Face polishing machines use a series of grinding, sanding and polishing discs to remove material from a gemstone. Each disc is finer and less abrasive than the previous one, so each disc produces more of a sanding, smoothing or polishing effect than the disc before it.

We will describe the different types of discs in the order they are used. Notice that each type of disc often has a specific color; we list the most commonly available colors for the given type of disc. With that said, disc colors can change, so the most important thing to understand is the numerical mesh of the grinding materials on the surface of the disc.

Ultra-Coarse Rough Grinding Disc (optional)

A silver disc with very coarse diamond abrasives, rated at 80–100 mesh. This disc is optional and should be used with care, as it can cause deep grooves and scratches in a stone; these can be difficult to remove in subsequent grinding stages. One valuable function that the ultra-coarse disc performs is chamfering and doming larger stones, a process that we will discuss later in the chapter.

Rough Grinding Disc

A silver disc with coarse diamond abrasives, rated at 180 mesh. This disc will be your workhorse for chamfering and doming smaller stones and cabochons. And if you've used an ultra-coarse grinding disc on a stone, this grinding disc will be used to remove the deeper scratches made by the ultra-coarse grind. This disc is a close equivalent to the coarse abrasive grit used in the first stage of tumble polishing.

Sanding Disc

A brown disc that is used to remove surface scratches and grooves caused by the grinding discs; it is also used to finely contour the gemstone surface.

Smoothing Discs

A set of two discs, one red and one blue, that are covered with diamond abrasives and are rated at 600 and 1,200 mesh, respectively. These discs remove tiny residual scratches, perform surface smoothing, and ultimately prepare the surface of the stones for polishing. Note that there are additional smoothing discs that can be used in sequence, but they are truly for ultra-high-grade stones that warrant the extra time and investment to obtain super-gloss finishes. In most cases, these discs aren't required.

Polishing Disc

A white absorbent disc used to apply polishing paste to gemstones, creating a high-gloss finish. The polishing paste itself consists of small diamond particles.

Polishing Paste

There are various gradients of diamond polishing paste, but a single 14,000-mesh gradient is usually sufficient.

Diamond Extender Fluid

Applied in conjunction with the diamond paste, this fluid helps coat the diamond paste to the polishing disc. This leads to less waste and helps you polish more stones with one application of polishing paste. The extender fluid also acts as a coolant and lubricant. (**Note:** Never run water on the polishing disc; we will remind you of this in the process steps below.)

HELPFUL TIP: Like diamond saw blades, the abrasive materials coated onto the grinding, sanding and polishing discs eventually wear down and need to be replaced. Usually you can obtain hundreds of hours of use from them and produce many beautiful display specimens before needing to replace them.

Coolants/Lubricants

Flat-laps require coolants, which also serve as lubricants. The machine we recommend uses water, which is supplied through a small plastic feeder tube. This tube is connected to a cup that sits above the sanding surface. Excess water drains off the edge of the rotating grinding disc into the base of the unit, and out through another plastic tube into a tub or a 5-gallon bucket on the floor.

Safety note: Never grind or sand your stones without water dripping onto the grinding disc. This saves wear and tear on the grinding discs, produces better results, and it reduces the amount of potentially harmful rock dust produced. There is a serious health condition known as silicosis that results from breathing in excessive amounts of rock dust. Use of lubricants when cutting and grinding is the most important way to minimize the chances of developing this condition. However, remember that you will not use water with the polishing disc, as this will ruin the disc. And while you don't sand or grind with the polishing disc, it does produce microscopic particles of polishing diamonds. Therefore, we also strongly recommend having a good ventilating fan. As another precaution, you can use a respirator or mask to further reduce the possibility of breathing in either rock dust or diamond particles.

Additional Equipment and Supplies

Plastic Trays

A set of five small plastic trays helps you keep track of the stones you are polishing in each face polishing stage; again, we strongly recommend processing stones together as a group through the successive stages. This means that you don't have to switch back and forth between grinding and polishing discs and helps you to get in a rhythm with the whole process.

Bucket or Pail

A 5-gallon pail set on the floor on an old bath towel catches the water draining out of the base of the face polishing machine when it's running. Empty the pail periodically, and be sure to empty it outdoors. Emptying it down an interior drain leads to major plumbing problems.

Dish Rack

A cheap plastic dish rack and a small hand towel are helpful, as they will help you store your grinding, sanding and polishing discs. Plus, keeping your discs in an upright position allows them to dry between uses and maximizes their product life. Lay a small hand towel over the top of your discs when you are done working. This prevents dust (or oil spray from your rock saw) from falling on your discs and decreasing their useful life. Pay particular attention to protecting the polishing disc; the extender fluid used on the disc is an oil-based compound that attracts dust and dirt. Keep this disc stored in a large manila business envelope and keep it there whenever it's not in use.

Magnifying Glass

A 5x magnifying glass, preferably with a small, embedded LED light, works great for inspecting your stones.

Tissue or Towels
Non-scratch tissue or soft, cotton dish towels are necessary for drying the stones prior to inspection.

Lamp
A desk lamp with a medium-high wattage lightbulb provides close-in light while grinding, polishing and inspecting your work.

Gallon Jug
A gallon jug is handy for refilling the water cup.

Choosing the Right Gemstones to Face Polish

Before you start polishing, you need to choose the right gemstones. There are two types of stones you can face polish. One option is to start with a whole or rough stone that has a reasonably even surface and some nice color and pattern exposed; a stone with an even and slightly rounded surface is a great fit because you don't need to do an excessive amount of grinding.

You can also face polish whole stones that either lack a visible pattern or stones that are deeply pitted or have obvious surface flaws, but before you can polish these stones, you must cut them using a lapidary saw.

Before getting into the details of operating the machine, you need to know how to select stones that will produce high-quality polished specimens.

Choosing Whole Stones

Let's talk about whole stones first—whole stones are simply natural stones that have not been cut using a lapidary saw. When face polishing whole stones, your goal is to produce a nicely curved surface. This is commonly referred to as dome polishing, because of the domed (curved) surface that results. While you can achieve a nicely curved dome when starting with a flat stone, with a whole stone you can achieve this doming effect faster because you won't need to cut the stone first. Dome polishing a whole stone is easiest if the stone has the following features:

Minimal depth variation: If there is more than $^1/_8$–$^1/_4$" of stone that needs to be ground away to obtain a smooth surface, you'll spend much more time than you probably have the patience for. This will also wear out your grinding discs more quickly. Stones with jagged points or deep pits are good candidates for face cutting, then polishing. Face cutting is done with a lapidary saw and results in a flat surface that can then be domed, ground and polished.

Exposed surface colors and patterns: If you cannot readily see the color and pattern on a stone, you will spend too much time grinding away the rough outer surface. Such stones may be good candidates for face cutting.

Lack of deep fractures: Even though a stone may have a reasonably flat or nicely contoured surface, and nice colors and patterns, it might also contain surface fractures that also go deeper into the stone. If a stone has a fracture that appears to extend beneath the surface of the stone, wet the stone and shine a bright light on it. If the fracture appears to penetrate below the surface, the stone can't be polished right away, as it likely needs to be face cut first. If the fracture appears to go deep into the stone, cutting it might be worthwhile, though it's possible the stone could be worthless for lapidary purposes if the fracture(s) spoils the beauty of the stone.

Some Examples of Whole Stones

These two stones exhibit sharp dips from the highest to the lowest points on the stones' surfaces, probably measuring $^1/_4$–$^1/_2$" in depth. There are also some significant fractures that appear to go beneath the visible surface. They would be

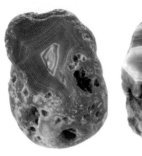 

good candidates for face cutting before face polishing.

The two stones at left have ridges that will require some grinding, but the darker stone has minimal surface-depth variation and even some natural rounding that will provide a nice doming contour. On these stones, there's lots of beautiful pattern already exposed and minimal surface fracturing. These stones can almost certainly be dome polished without face cutting them first.

Cutting Stones for Face Polishing

Moving on to cut stones, it's less about selecting stones with the right surface features and more about cutting your stones in a way that makes face polishing easier. While you'll also want to select stones that have pleasing colors and patterns, it's important to keep in mind that saw cuts leave behind grooves, surface dimples and excess stone near the end of the saw cut. Therefore, when you are cutting stones for face polishing, it's critical that you follow all the tips in the Cutting chapter (see page 71). By following those tips you'll substantially minimize the extra grinding that would be needed to get a perfectly polished face. Regardless of how clean your saw cut is, for face-cut stones you will almost always use the chamfering technique that we describe to bring the surface to a domed shape, and this will also remove significant saw cut marks and dimples.

HELPFUL TIP: For reference, you shouldn't try to face polish stones with more than 2–3 square inches of surface area. Stones that are larger than this require high-end (costly) commercial grinding and polishing machines.

Determining How to Face Polish a Stone

In some ways, face polishing gemstones is similar to cutting them. When face polishing, you need to select the surface you want to polish and how best to approach it. As with cutting, this is somewhat intuitive, which means there is no perfect way to decide how to orient your gemstone on the grinding disc. As you gain experience, you will develop your own techniques. Just like with cutting, when you first get started face polishing, it's good to practice on lower-quality materials before starting to polish higher-grade gemstones. This will get you comfortable with using the lapidary sander and help you practice important operations, such as initiating the grinding operation and rocking, rotating and sanding the stone. Below are some general guidelines to help determine the best polishing surface and angle for your gemstones.

A Domed Polish vs. Polishing a Flat Stone

When face polishing, you need to decide whether you want your polished surface to be flat or domed. In general, with a domed surface, it is much easier to obtain a uniform high-gloss polish. It is simpler because a curved area exposes less surface area to the disc at one time; this allows you to apply more pressure to that area. In fact, if you're polishing a curved surface, you can apply up to ten times

dome polished   flat-surface face polished

as much pressure as you could to an entire flat surface of a stone, helping to remove even small surface dimples. Therefore, the bulk of our discussion will focus on creating dome-polished surfaces (which will also be referred to in the Cabochon Making chapter, page 133).

Maximize the Most Beautiful Features

Look for the most striking color or pattern combinations that are already exposed on the stone, but keep in mind that you will probably want to avoid starting in areas of the stone that would require extensive grinding.

Bring the Surface to an Even Level and Remove Flaws

If the gemstone you want to face polish has an uneven surface, or significant surface flaws or blemishes, the first thing you need to do is address these issues. Protruding material needs to be ground away to make a nearly even surface. Grooves, pits and valleys are removed by grinding away the excess surface material surrounding them. (If there is more than $^1/_8$–$^1/_4$" of material to remove, it's better to face cut the stone than try to grind away that much material.) Once you have achieved a nearly even surface, or if you started with a stone that has been face cut, you can start to create a domed or contoured surface.

Before You Start

Checking Your Work

It might seem unusual that we are telling you about checking your work before you get started, **but it is so critical to success in face polishing that we place this information upfront!**

Once you think you're finished with each face polishing stage, it's time to clean your gemstones and inspect your work. Before you can inspect your gemstones, you need to clean them. Cleaning is simple—just dip them in your water supply cup and rub them gently with a soft cloth rag to remove any grit or ground rock. Then give them a moment to air dry so there is no remaining moisture to mask small scratches and surface imperfections.

After that, it's time to inspect your gemstones. We mentioned earlier that you can turn out nicely face-polished stones in less than an hour. But if we can give you one piece of advice—if you rush from stage to stage, you will get to the end and wonder why your stones have only a dull glow instead of the high-gloss shine you expected. A good inspection is truly the secret to face polishing! After you finish a step in the grinding, sanding, smoothing or polishing process, stop and take a look at your work, and if necessary, revisit that step. To make things easier for you, we'll be including inspection tips at the end of each stage. When it comes to these inspections, we cannot over-emphasize the importance of attention to detail; inspections enable you to check your work, thereby ensuring a higher-quality result.

How to Hold and Move Your Gemstones

In order to get the most out of your machine and maximize the lifespan of your grinding, sanding and polishing discs, you need to know how to hold, position and move your gemstones. We recommend holding your gemstone with the first four fingers of your dominant hand, as this will give you a good amount of control.

In addition, there are a few motions that come in handy when grinding, sanding and polishing. When you're grinding and sanding a stone, we recommend gently rocking the gemstone. Rocking a stone reduces the amount of surface area in contact with the sander, as it keeps a flat spot from developing where the stone is in contact with the disc. Rocking dramatically increases the amount of

pressure on the surface that is being worked, which speeds up the operation and reduces wear on your discs. Additionally, the rocking motion helps develop a dome or contour on the face of the gemstone.

When you're rocking a stone, you should also gradually rotate it (either clockwise or counterclockwise); this evens out the grinding or sanding process and will create a smoothly contoured dome shape. If you simply rock the stone back and forth without rotating it, you might end up with a less pleasing tube-like shape.

Starting the Machine

Now that you know the basics about face polishing, you're almost ready to start. Before you start, however, always fill the machine's water supply cup to the top, and ensure that the drain tube is going into your 5-gallon bucket. (**Note:** Never start the water drip until the machine is running; if water drips down the shaft where the discs are bolted on, it can ruin the sander's motor.) After that, you need to place the appropriate disc onto the sander. To do so, simply unscrew the top bolt, place your disc on the spindle and tighten the top bolt.

Now you're ready to start the machine. The flat-lap sander we recommend is controlled through a variable-speed dial on the front of the machine, making it incredibly easy to operate. Almost all of the time, we recommend running the machine at nearly full speed, as this will make it easier to give a uniform finish to your stones. And it allows you to apply the maximum amount of pressure without slowing the rotation speed of the disc, which can result in additional abrasions or flat spots on the stone's surface.

Once the disc is spinning, turn the small knob on the water supply tube until water is dripping at about two drops per second. The end of the water supply tube should be about even with where the grinding abrasive begins at the center of the disc. The entire surface of the disc should become damp.

Getting Started

Stage 1: Creating a Smooth Domed or Contoured Surface

For whole stones with a nicely rounded surface, you can begin working the stone against either the ultra-coarse grinding disc or the rough grinding disc. Your choice of disc depends on the size of the stone and amount of material you need to remove. For example, larger stones or stones with more significant surface variations suggest using the ultra-rough disc, while smaller stones, cabochons, and stones of lower hardness suggest using the standard rough disc.

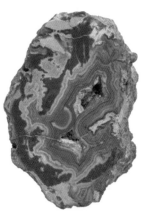

face-cut stone
before chamfering

The first step in doming or contouring a stone that has been face cut, or that otherwise has a relatively flat surface, is to create a beveled edge around the face of the entire stone; this is called a chamfer. For larger stones and stones with deeper surface indentations, more material will need to be removed, so you will need to create a chamfer that is wider and

start

chamfered

domed

more steeply angled, say at a 45-degree angle to the face. For this you will most likely want to use the ultra-coarse disc. For smaller stones and cabochons, the chamfer will be relatively narrow and at a lower angle, say 30 degrees, and we recommend using the standard rough grinding disc, especially since these stones are more delicate.

HELPFUL TIP: Larger gemstones need a deeper and wider chamfer. This is where the ultra-rough grinding disc really comes in handy, as it quickly removes larger amounts of stone and shapes highly uneven surfaces quickly and efficiently. When using the ultra-coarse disc, be careful not to apply too much pressure, because it will leave deeper scratches in your stones and these can take a lot of grinding to fix.

To create the chamfer, place the edge of the face of the stone against the grinding disc and begin rocking (tilting) the stone up and down as you slowly rotate the stone. Work all the way around the stone until you have a uniform angle. For larger stones, you'll repeat this process a few times (2–3) in order to create a wide enough chamfer. These larger stones also require a more pronounced chamfer angle, and this often involves rocking the stone quite a bit to grind away the additional flat surface material.

You're finished when you have a chamfer that is wide and deep enough that by the time the stone is smoothly domed from the center of the face to the chamfered edge, all surface-depth variations and flaws have been removed.

After creating the chamfer around the circumference of the stone, begin to work your gemstone into a domed shape. To do so, begin by rocking the stone gradually back and forth while also applying significant pressure against the grinding disc. You can exert quite a lot of force without slowing the speed of the disc, and as long as you're rocking the stone, you won't damage it. Then, gradually rotate the stone clockwise or counterclockwise, while also rocking the stone. The gradual rotation around the entire surface of the stone creates a smooth sloping dome rather than just a half-tube-shaped surface (which is not a naturally pleasing contour).

If you have been using the ultra-rough disc, you should now switch to the rough grinding disc to smooth out some of the heavier scratches that come from the ultra-rough disc. Repeat the rocking and rotation actions across the entire domed surface of the stone one or two times, and then inspect your work to ensure you have removed any deep scratches or grooves. This activity will also remove most of the flat spots and angular faceting, so that the surface is nicely rounded.

You're finished when your whole stone or cabochon has a nicely contoured dome shape and there are no significant surface indentations that are visible to the naked eye (i.e., they are less than $^1/_{16}$" in depth). The surface of the stone will be scratchy and rough, but this isn't a concern; subsequent sanding and smoothing operations will remove the scratches and minor surface flaws.

HELPFUL TIP: There are some softer materials, such as turquoise and Apache tears, that require less force than harder stones, like agate or quartz, so take this into consideration as you polish different types of gemstone materials. In fact, we recommend not using the ultra-coarse grinding disc with these softer materials. Instead, use the rough grinding disc in its place.

Checking Your Work

Reminder: When checking your work, always dip your stone in water and then clean and dry it with a soft cloth first. Allow the stone to completely dry as moisture will mask some surface scratches and flaws.

Part 1: Chamfering (optional for whole stones that weren't face cut)

You're finished when the stone exhibits a uniform chamfer (beveled edge) around the circumference of the stone.

after chamfering

Part 2: Doming

You're finished when the surface is uniformly round and smooth, and there are no major pits or surface-depth variations greater than $^1/_{16}$"; the surface will be visibly rough and coarse when dry, with noticeable scratches.

after doming

Part 3: Smoothing

You're finished when the surface is uniformly smooth but dull and a bit scratchy in some spots. The surface of the stone will be nicely rounded with minimal flat spots, or faceting.

If you are dome polishing a whole stone, you will have a nicely contoured surface that follows the outline of the stone and gently rises to a dome toward the middle of the stone's surface. It takes some time to master this, but it's worth it; there is a distinct difference between a nicely shaped dome and a stone that was just rocked back and forth at one angle.

after coarse sanding

Stage 2: Coarse Sanding

Sanding doesn't remove any significant amount of material, so before beginning this stage, you need to be sure that you've gotten the stone down to the shape and surface contour that you want your stone to have when it is finished. The sanding disc removes any remaining sharp edges or angles left from rough grinding and also removes any scratches that are visible to the naked eye.

When it comes to actually sanding and smoothing, you use the same techniques as in the grinding stage. Gradually rotate the stone clockwise or counterclockwise, while also rocking it. Be sure to move around the entire surface of the stone. (**Note:** When rocking a stone during sanding, you can rock the stone back and forth more quickly than in the grinding stage.)

Cleaning, inspecting and drying your gemstones is very important during the sanding stage, as this is your last chance to remove any significant flaws left in the stone. You will probably do this 2–3 times. This helps you ensure your gemstone has a uniform surface texture that is smooth and nicely contoured.

Checking Your Work

You're finished when the stones have a smooth, uniform surface and even the hint of a soft glow, and there are no pits or surface-depth variations visible to the human eye. (When we say no pits or dimples, we mean zero! Otherwise, they will show up as ugly dull spots on your polished gemstones and cabochons.)

There must also be zero scratches or grooves left from the rough grinding phase or from sawing (again, we mean zero!).

And the edges of the stone must be smoothed-in with the overall surface, with no flat spots or sharp edges.

If you have not achieved these results, either go back to the coarse grinding disc to remove the flaws or continue with the sanding operation until you get to the desired outcome. Whatever you do, don't skip ahead to the next stage; this will only waste your time and you'll have to circle back through the last several stages a second time!

Stage 3: Fine Sanding and Smoothing

The fine smoothing disc eliminates scratches on the stone. When you're sanding and smoothing your gemstones you employ the same basic techniques that you used while grinding (rocking and rotating a gemstone while pressing it against the polishing disc). In this phase, however, you'll exert somewhat less pressure and need to pay more attention to detail in order to ensure that you cover

after fine sanding

the entire surface of the stone; when you're done, the stone will have an even finish that is slightly glossy. You should only have to spend a minute or two on this stage.

As with the sanding stage, you will want to stop a couple of times with each stone to clean, dry and inspect the stone under a bright light to verify the surface is uniformly smooth.

Checking Your Work

You're finished when the stones have a uniform smooth surface and a soft glow across the entire face or dome, and there are no dull or slightly scratchy spots.

Stage 4: Ultra-Fine Smoothing

The ultra-fine smoothing disc prepares the stone to receive polishing compound. The polishing techniques in this stage are similar to those in previous stages; you rock and rotate the stone while holding it against the sanding disc. Just as with fine smoothing and sanding, you should exert somewhat less pressure and cover the entire surface of the stone. This results in an

after ultra-fine smoothing

even and glossy finish that indicates the stone is ready for polishing. You should only have to spend a minute or two on this stage.

With that said, it's prudent to stop a couple of times with each stone to clean, dry and inspect the stone under a bright light to verify that the surface texture is uniform and smooth.

HELPFUL TIP: When you first get started with face polishing, you might be inclined to rush this stage, but resist the temptation, because this last step is what sets you up for a killer, high-gloss shine vs. a nice, but sub-par, polish.

Checking Your Work

You're finished when your stones or cabochons have a uniform soft glow across the entire face or dome and there are no dull spots; many beginners might think they are done when they are finished with this stage. (And if you want a satin finish on your stones or cabs, you actually are done!)

Stage 5: Polishing

Polishing is the last stage in the face polishing process. Whereas all of the previous stages are about removing material, shaping the stone and preparing the surface of the stone for polishing, this stage actually applies the specialized polishing compounds that give your gemstone that high-gloss shine.

To polish a stone, you first need to attach the special polishing disc. (**Note:** The polishing stage does not use water, so be sure to have your water drip turned off before you start.) Instead of using water, you need to inject 5-8 small streaks of polishing compound onto the disc using the injection tube. This amount of diamond paste should last for 3-5 stones depending on the size of the stones or cabochons. Use your forefinger to lightly spread the polishing compound onto the cloth material that covers the disc; it will not cover the entire surface of the disc. Next, drip some of the diamond extender fluid onto the disc. This will keep the polishing compound from drying out too quickly and coming off of the disc as a fine powder.

Now it's time to start polishing. Start the machine and hold the stone against the polishing disc. (**Note:** You don't need to exert nearly as much pressure when polishing; if you use too much, polishing compound will come off the disc too quickly.) When polishing, gradually rotate the stone clockwise or counterclockwise while also rocking the stone, moving around the entire surface of the stone. Note that polishing doesn't require the rapid back-and-forth sanding motion necessary in the other sanding and smoothing stages. Use a soft cloth every 5-10 seconds to gently rub away excess polishing compound from your gemstone and inspect your results. Polishing a stone only takes about a minute, much less than the previous stages.

Checking Your Work

You're finished when you look at your polished stones and they look back at you and smile! We really mean it: There is no second-guessing the beaming shine that tells you "that's a job well done!" Your finished gemstones will have a consistent high-gloss polish and no dull or uneven spots.

after polishing

Remember . . .

- The ultra-coarse rough grinding stage should be performed with care; otherwise, it's easy to create deep scratches in your gemstones that are difficult to remove. Consider face cutting stones that have too much excess material or deep surface flaws before starting grinding operations.

- Inspecting stones carefully at the end of each processing stage is the "secret sauce" of polishing. Master this part of the process and you are well on your way to creating beautiful, high-gloss gems.

- Process your gemstones in batches and set them in a series of plastic trays to represent the next stage to be performed. This will dramatically improve your productivity and help your work be more consistent.

- With each processing stage, your excitement will mount. Avoid the temptation to rush ahead, and be sure to make sure you are truly finished with that stage by inspecting your stones carefully.

- Take good care of your grinding, sanding and polishing discs and they will give you years of good service. Keep them upright in a dish rack, and keep them covered with a small dish towel to protect them from dust, oil spray and debris, which will reduce their effectiveness.

- To get a nicely contoured dome shape on your stones, follow the natural surface contours of the stone as much as possible as you sand the stone by rocking, rotating and moving it back and forth. When grinding and shaping, avoid straight lines and half-tube shapes, which are less pleasing to the eye than dome shapes.

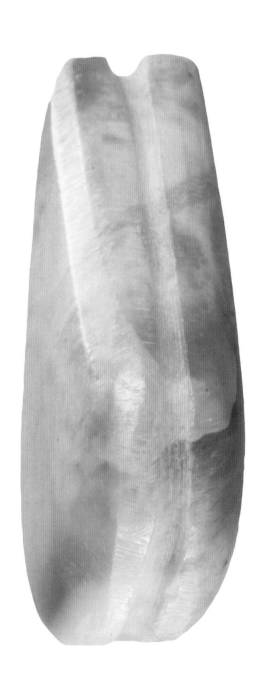

Routing

What It Is

Lapidary routing creates a shallow groove around the outside edge of a gemstone pendant. The groove provides a place to conceal the wire wrapping used to attach the stone to a necklace or bracelet chain. This technique provides an alternative to drilling into or through your gemstone, which is tedious work and often comes with the risk of damaging the stone.

Process Overview

The routing process that we describe in this chapter simply involves attaching a router bit (and a sponge), starting the router, and then grooving the stone around its entire circumference.

Equipment and Lapidary Supplies

Routing require a lapidary grinder and a diamond-coated routing bit.

Process Highlights

Successful routing involves holding the stone with consistent, moderate pressure against the router bit. As you proceed, use a slow side-to-side swiveling motion, with careful examination of your work as to groove depth to ensure successful results.

Time Requirements

Routing is one of the quickest of the lapidary techniques discussed in this book. For a standard-shaped cabochon, such as an oval shape, it might take only a couple minutes to create a complete edge grooving. Shapes with sharper inside and outside corners could take up to 10 minutes.

Recommended Equipment

For edging and routing, we recommend using the Gryphon Gryphette grinder. This machine is made primarily for people who work with glass and produce works such as stained glass, but it's also perfectly suited for creating a shallow groove along the edge of your natural-shape gemstone slabs or shaped cabochons.

Setup and Operation

The machine we recommend is very quiet and nearly mess free, so there are no special setup or operating considerations. This lapidary router uses water as a coolant and a lubricant, so there is no oil to be concerned with. Nonetheless, if you wish, you can set up a drip station for your router. A drip station consists of a small stand with small tub of water and a drip hose; this is similar to the standard setup that comes with flat lapidary sanders. This provides a more steady flow of water than the standard router setup. A drip station also reduces the amount of rock dust that is generated when routing, edging and grinding gemstones.

HELPFUL TIP: If you have a larger slab or cab that you are working with, consider stopping at the halfway point for a few minutes and letting the bit cool down. This keeps the router bit from overheating and burning away too much of the diamond coating.

A Few Important Notes

- In order to cut a shallow groove into your gemstones, they need to be thick enough to handle the cut. Generally speaking, slabs and cabs need to have a minimum thickness of $^1/_8$–$^3/_{16}$".

- Lapidary routing can be easily performed on both natural-shape gemstone slabs and shaped cabochons, but if there are any tight cuts or corners, the router bit may not be able to fully penetrate into those narrow indentations, so it's often better to drill or wire wrap such stones.

- **Safety note:** If you are working with gemstone materials that generate a significant amount of rock dust, consider setting up a drip station to ensure a steady drip of water onto the sponge behind the router bit. There is a serious health condition known as silicosis that results from breathing in excessive amounts of rock dust. Use of lubricants when cutting and grinding is the most important way to minimize chances of developing this condition. We also strongly recommend having a good ventilating fan. As another precaution, you can use a respirator or mask to further reduce the possibility of breathing in either rock dust or diamond particles.

Getting Started

Step 1: Attaching a Bit and a Sponge

Begin by attaching the router bit that you'll be using, and then fill the water reservoir below the edging table according to the manufacturer's instructions. Then, place a small square of a common household sponge (we recommend cutting a square to fit) so that it fits snugly between the vertical plastic guides directly behind the router bit. And with that, you're ready to get started!

Step 2: Edging the Stone

After you've selected a cabochon, turn on the router and lay the stone on the router surface. If you have set up a water drip stand and container, begin the water drip and set it at about one drip per second. Holding the stone firmly with the fingertips of both hands,

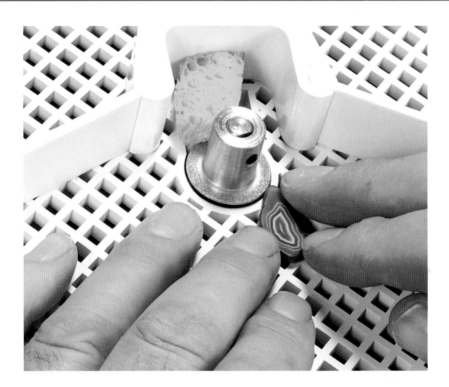

gently slide the stone up against the router bit and apply moderate pressure while swiveling the stone slightly from side to side and gradually rotating the stone either clockwise or counterclockwise.

HELPFUL TIP: The diamond coating on router bits is thin and will wear away quickly if you exert too much pressure. Use only moderate pressure and a gentle swiveling motion to reduce wear on the bit and extend the life of the diamond coating.

Step 3: Checking Your Work

Since each type of gemstone material is different, you should stop and inspect the stone after the first few swivels to see if you are getting the correct groove depth. Like drill bits, the router bits have a relatively short life, so you want to cut grooves only as deep as necessary. The grooves only need to be deep enough to hold the wire that'll be surrounding the stone. In general, you should cut the groove to about $1/32$", as that will conceal the wire and also allow it to grip firmly.

Step 4: Getting to a Finished Product

After verifying that you are getting the groove depth that you want, continue alternating between swiveling and rotating the stone. Continue along the outside of the whole stone. After working around the whole piece, inspect the groove all the way around, as there will invariably be some spots where the groove is too shallow. Rework those specific sections and then stop to inspect until you are satisfied that you have a nice uniform groove.

Another Use for a Lapidary Router

One nice additional feature of lapidary routers is that they can be used for grinding chamfers (beveled edges) onto your cabochons (see page 101); this is a precursor to grinding the stone down to a domed surface. If you want to use your router for this purpose, you

can purchase additional bits for your router that are used for grinding gemstone materials. In order to see what you prefer, consider experimenting with the lapidary router and see how it compares to a flat lapidary sander.

chamfering router bit

edging router bits

Remember . . .

- If you will be working with gemstone materials that generate a significant amount of rock dust (especially any type that might be noxious), consider setting up a drip station to ensure a steady drip of water onto the sponge behind the router bit.

- Make sure that your natural-shape gemstone slabs or shaped cabochons are at least $^1/_8$–$^3/_{16}$" thick in order to allow the router bit to grip firmly into the stone.

- The diamond coating on router bits is thin and will wear away quickly if you exert too much pressure. Use only moderate pressure and a gentle swiveling motion to reduce excess wear on the bits and extend the life of their diamond coating.

Drilling

What It Is

Drilling gemstones is somewhat of an advanced lapidary operation that is used to create a hole through or into gemstone pendants. It's possible to substitute other operations for drilling, such as wire wrapping. However the drilling operation is still widely used by lapidary artists, and while it's not complicated, it does require considerable patience and use of fine motor skills.

Process Overview

There are two different ways to drill a stone. One way is to lay the stone flat and then drill all the way through it; this is generally referred to as face drilling. The other option, referred to as top drilling, involves drilling partway into the top of the stone to allow insertion of a jewelry post, which is then fastened with an adhesive.

Equipment and Supplies

Drilling stones requires a specialized lapidary drill press and diamond-coated drill bits. These machines allow for a high level of precision and have a high-torque, variable-speed motor, which is required to efficiently drill through valuable gems. They also feature coolant systems that prevent your diamond drill bits from getting burned out too quickly and reduce chipping and fracturing of the gemstone materials.

Process Highlights

The most important thing to keep in mind is that drilling very hard gemstones is entirely different than working with ordinary household drills. Instead of applying constant pressure, when using a lapidary drill it's essential to use a light-touch press-and-release technique.

Time Requirements

Drilling is a relatively quick process, taking about 3-5 minutes per pendant stone. It might take more or less time depending on the thickness of the stone when face drilling or the depth of the hole needed when top drilling. The hardness of the gemstone material is also a factor. Softer stones like turquoise take less time, while harder stones like agate take longer.

HELPFUL TIP: Some consider drilling to be more of an advanced technique. While we heartily encourage you to try it out, if it's not for you, there are some alternatives to drilling. Jewelry pieces can be made by routing (see page 111) or by wire wrapping (see page 160). Drilling is also unnecessary for making products such as standard-size cabochons (made using a template) that will be placed into form-fitting jewelry settings (see page 148).

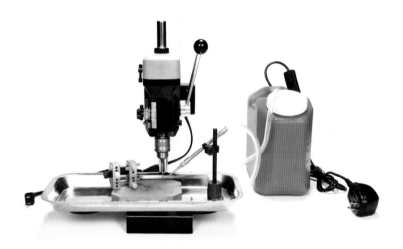

Recommended Equipment

Many people believe that hardware and home improvement grade drills and drill bits can be used on gemstones, but these tools are only a recipe for broken and chipped stones and ruined drill bits. Also, while there are commercial drill presses that can be adapted to lapidary drilling processes, you'll be better served to use a machine that has been purpose built for lapidary work. These machines aren't more expensive, they just have the kinds of controls you'll find useful for drilling hard gemstone materials.

We recommend the MicroLux 3-Speed Mini Drill Press used in conjunction with the MicroFlow Coolant System, both from Micro-Mark. Other quality drill press brands are Foredom and Covington Engineering.

Setup and Operation

Lapidary drill presses are very quiet, and if you use the coolant-delivery system we recommend, they don't create much of a mess. They are also highly portable, so you can set them up in any well-lit area. It helps to have a bright desk lamp nearby to make inspecting your progress easier.

Additional Equipment and Supplies

Hollow-core Diamond Drill Bits
There are numerous types of lapidary drill bits, and you might even find some that are silicon carbide. We strongly recommend diamond-tipped hollow-core drill bits. They last the longest (though this is relative) and offer the most precise drilling. The recommended size range for most gemstone drilling is 1.0–2.5 millimeters, with a maximum of 4 millimeters.

Cooling Fluid
Lapidary suppliers sell coolant mixtures for use with diamond drill bits. These can be diluted with water and put into the cooling reservoir, which usually consists of a 2–3 gallon jug with a delivery hose that ends with a small plastic nozzle. We strongly recommend that you use such lubricants, which are specifically formulated to reduce heat buildup and will extend the life of your drill bits.

Extra Fine Spray Nozzles
These attach to the end of the coolant delivery tube and spray a small jet of coolant onto the gemstones while you're drilling.

Cutting Board
When drilling, we recommend doing so on a small, hard cutting board.

Mini-Vise
When you're top drilling, it's helpful to have a small vise to hold gemstones steady while drilling.

Stainless Steel Tray

A small stainless steel tray holds the cutting board and catches excess coolant runoff.

Soft Clay

When you're drilling through the face of a stone, it's often helpful to set it in soft clay. This holds it steady while you're drilling. This also reduces the "breakout factor" on the reverse side of the stone. The clay is set onto the hardwood block, and then the gemstone is pressed into the clay.

Cloth Shop Rags

These are useful for cleaning up spills and for wiping off stones during drilling.

Two Types of Drilling

Face Drilling

Face drilling means drilling all the way through a jewelry pendant or cabochon while it is lying flat. The stone is held steady by pressing it into soft clay on top of a small cutting board. We recommend against drilling through gemstone pieces that are thicker than $1/8$,

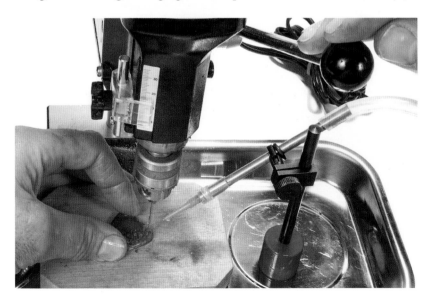

especially when it comes to very hard stones, such as agate or quartz. If your jewelry pendant can be worn to display both sides, you should drill the stone partway through from each side in order to avoid breakout on the backside of the stone as the drill bit comes through. This means that before you start drilling you need to carefully mark a point on the front and back side of the jewelry pendant that will ensure the two holes line up exactly. Alternatively, you can wait until you are partially through the drilling operation on the first side, then hold the stone to your desk lamp and make a mark where you see light through the back of the stone.

Top Drilling

Top drilling means drilling a hole approximately $1/4$" into the top of the gemstone material so that you can glue a jewelry post into the top of the stone. The post will usually have a loop so that a chain or cord necklace can be placed through it. During drilling, the stones are held steady by a miniature vise that sits atop a small hardwood block. If you will be doing a lot of top drilling, you might even go as far as to permanently secure the mini-vise to the wooden block to further reduce any movement while drilling. When top drilling,

you need to carefully inspect the stone to ensure there aren't existing fractures; these fractures can cause breaks during the drilling process. You also need to ensure that the top of the stone is wide (thick) enough; generally speaking, the surface of the stone that you will be drilling into should be at least two times the diameter of the hole you're planning on drilling.

HELPFUL TIP: The top drilling method can also be used to make jewelry beads. However, we recommend that you only use softer gemstone materials for making beads. If you use harder materials (such as agate), it's difficult to drill completely through them.

Critical Drilling Tips

Don't Drill Polished Stones

We recommend that you drill stones that aren't yet fully ground and polished. Using stones that have passed through the medium-grind stage is best (see page 54); if the stones have already been through the fine grind or full polish stage, it makes it more difficult to obtain the initial drilling impression, and this also means you won't be able to fine grind or polish away any visible imperfections caused by drilling.

Drilling Stone is Different than Drilling Wood

When it comes to drilling, using a lapidary drill is entirely different than working with ordinary woodworking drills or power tools. In a woodworking drill, the drill immediately "bites" into the surface of the wood and you achieve the desired drilling depth by exerting consistent downward pressure (as opposed to the press-and-release technique we'll describe on page 128). Because drilling stones is entirely different, you should not attempt to use a lapidary drill in the same way you would use a household drill. (This can be tough to do at first if you're an experienced woodworker.)

Keep an Eye on the Drill Bits

As you are drilling, you also need to monitor for drill bit wear. An experienced operator can drill 10-20 gemstones with one diamond bit. A less experienced operator might only get 1-3 drilled stones.

Regardless of your skill level, you need to listen and watch for signs that the drill bit is spent (i.e., all of the diamond abrasive has worn off). While drilling you'll notice a small but continual outflow of stone slurry coming from the point of impact. If you stop seeing this slurry and/or the drill bit starts to make more of a whining sound, then it's likely that the bit is worn out. And if your drill bit is glowing orange-red, you have probably ruined your gemstone piece because all of the diamond drill bit coating has melted and is now at the bottom of the drill impression.

Getting Started

Step 1: Securing Your Specimen

Because lapidary drills can easily cause heat to build up, it's critical to ensure that your gemstone is well secured before drilling, as any excess vibration or wobble in either the stone itself or the drill bit will lead to more friction and heat. We therefore recommend that your drill bit should only extend $^{1}/_{4}$–$^{1}/_{2}$" out of the drill chuck end.

HELPFUL TIP: If you want to hold the stone extra steady, you can set it in modeling clay, or dop wax that's attached to the hardwood block. For more information about dop wax, see the Cabochon Making chapter (page 133).

Step 2: Check the Drill Settings

Once you are ready to start drilling, you should set the drill press speed to the lowest possible setting that will produce results; our general recommendation is approximately 1,000 RPM. This low RPM setting is in fact what separates good-quality lapidary drill presses from ordinary drill presses, and is necessary to get the longest life out of your diamond-coated drill bits. While you can drill at much higher speeds, the lower the RPM, the lower the amount of heat buildup. Finally, before you begin drilling, be sure to start the flow of lubricant spray. The lubricant should coat the point on the stone where you'll be drilling the hole. If you haven't used our recommended coolant setup, you'll need a spray bottle

to periodically spray the stone. Another way to cool and lubricate a stone is to immerse the stone completely in cooling lubricant inside of a small plastic tray. This method is generally effective but makes it harder to tell how drilling is going.

Step 3: Begin Drilling

To start drilling, slowly and carefully exert pressure onto the gemstone. The drill bit will likely dance or skitter around the smooth and wet surface of the stone, and your first instinct will be to press harder to try and get traction; this is the exact opposite of what you need to do! Instead of pushing even harder, let the drill bit do its work. You will know that you have created an initial impression when you begin to see a small amount of stone slurry

(powdered stone material mixed with lubricant), as shown in the photo at left, and when you start to hear a consistent drilling sound.

HELPFUL TIP: If you are getting too much vibration, the drill bit is telling you to ease back and apply less pressure until you've begun to penetrate the stone's surface. It might also be telling you that your drill bit is extended too far out of the drill chuck or that the stone itself is not being held securely enough for drilling.

Step 4: Press-and-Release

Once the drill has clearly begun to cut into the stone, you need to avoid another common instinct: driving the bit through the rest of the stone. Instead of doing that, press the bit down a little, then pull back, and then repeat this process. This will ensure you aren't overheating the tip of the drill bit and allows the cooling lubricant to flush the drill hole and cool the drill bit itself. You'll actually learn the press-and-release technique rather quickly once you get going, because if you're doing it incorrectly, you'll notice that your expensive diamond drill bits are burning out after drilling only 2–3 stones.

The press-and-release movement is actually more akin to a pulsing motion with one-second intervals: one second pressing the drill down into the stone, one second up. When you are first learning, you should literally count out loud, pressing down on the odd numbers, and lifting up off the stone completely on the even ones. For hard gemstone materials like agate and jasper, it takes about 100 presses to get all the way through the stone.

Step 5: Monitoring Your Progress

When Face Drilling

As you get into a rhythm of drilling, you need to continually monitor how far the drill bit is getting into the gemstone. For face drilled stones, you want to begin to ease up on the pressure as you get farther into the stone. This is true whether you'll be drilling all the way through the stone or flipping the stone over and drilling through from the opposite side.

Easing up on pressure has two advantages: If you're drilling all the way through a stone, it minimizes breakout on the reverse side of the stone. If you're going to be flipping the stone over, easing up on pressure prevents you from accidentally drilling all the way through and allows for a consistent, smooth hole on each side of the stone.

HELPFUL TIP: When in doubt, check your work. Always remember that when face drilling you can always stop drilling and hold the stone up to your desk lamp to evaluate your progress.

When Top Drilling

When it comes to top drilling, you don't have to worry about breakout or chipping. Instead, your primary concern is drilling only as deep as necessary to set your jewelry post and adhesive. This results in a more secure setting for your jewelry post and ensures that the cooling lubricant is getting to the tip of the drill bit (it can't if the drill bit is too deep in the stone), which ultimately limits the wear on your diamond drill bits.

Drilling Tips Summary
(photocopy for display in your workshop)

Remember . . .

- Only allow the bit to extend out of the drill as much as needed to achieve the depth of the hole that you'll be drilling. This reduces the wobble, and thus the heat builds up more slowly. Recommended is $1/4$–$1/2$".

- For stones that aren't flat, you'll need to secure them with something like soft molding clay or dop wax. Another great option is plumber's putty. Do not use Play-Doh!

- Choosing which side to drill into: If only one surface will be showing in your jewelry piece, start by drilling into the side that will show. For those that will have both surfaces displayed, it is best to drill from both sides; this eliminates the "breakout" effect that is common when you drill all the way through the stone.

- Drill at the slowest recommended speed possible, such as 1,000 RPM, as it keeps the heat to a minimum while drilling, thus reducing premature wear of the diamond abrasives on the tip of the drill bit.

- Drill your gemstones after they have completed the medium grind stage of face polishing or tumbling and before the fine grind and polishing stages. This makes it easier to create the initial "drilling impression" and allows you to smooth away any imperfections from the drilling process during the fine grind and polishing stages.

What It Is

Cabochon making involves several lapidary processes that convert rough gemstone materials into symmetrical shapes (an oval or a rectangle, for example) that are used to make jewelry pieces, such as necklaces, bracelets, cuff links, etc.

Process Overview

Making cabochons involves a number of lapidary techniques, such as cutting, grinding and dome polishing, that have already been covered in this book. The chart on page 137 lists the major steps required to make a cabochon and the chapter where each of these techniques is covered.

Equipment and Lapidary Supplies

Because making cabochons involves a number of different processes, it also requires the use of a number of machines. The only machine that we haven't already covered in other chapters is the dop pot. Dop pots heat up dopping wax, which is used to secure your gemstones to dop sticks, which you hold on to as you work with the stones. Creating cabochons also requires metal cabochon stencils, special stencil-marking pencils, methyl alcohol and an X-Acto knife.

Process Highlights

Since making cabochons is a time-intensive process, start by choosing high-quality gemstone materials. Also make sure to optimize the use of these stones by creating shapes that both use the best features of the stone and minimize waste. As time goes by and your skill progresses, begin to create free-form shapes rather than strict geometric shapes from stencils, making your creations truly personal!

Time Requirements

Making cabochons is the most time-consuming process in this book. On average, a simply shaped cab (such as an oval or rectangle) might take 10-15 minutes, and more complex shapes can take longer. However, you will be much more efficient and thereby reduce this time considerably when you do multiple stones in a batch, running each stone through Step 1 (stencil), then each stone through Step 2 (trim saw), etc., until the entire batch is complete.

Recommended Equipment

While there are other types of heating pots that can be used, lapidary dop pots are inexpensive, and they are expressly made to heat your dop wax to the perfect temperature range to melt but not boil or burn the wax, which would make it ineffective. Additionally, the dop pot shown has a flat rim around the edge of the pot that you can set your trim-cut cabochons onto and thus warm them up before attaching them to the dop stick. This helps to create a super-tight bond between the stone and the dop wax. Pictured is a popular high quality Dop Station.

Setup and Operation

Once again, many of the techniques necessary for creating cabochons are covered in prior chapters, so we'll focus on the additional techniques and tips that are essential to consistently creating high-quality cabochons.

When you're making cabochons, adequate lighting is absolutely key, because the process requires fine motor skills and a high degree of precision. We recommend working in an area that is well lit with natural light; we also recommend including a bright desk lamp in your immediate work area. In addition, your workspace should be in a clean and relatively dust-free area. While your lapidary operations will generate plenty of airborne dust and oil particles, a clean workspace will make dopping and polishing your cabochons easier.

Additional Equipment and Supplies

In addition to the lapidary supplies needed for the steps covered in previous chapters, for cabochon making you will also need:

Dop Wax

This wax is formulated specifically to create a hard bond between your gemstone materials and the dop sticks. It's relatively inexpensive, and it's therefore best to purchase dop wax rather than paraffin or candle wax.

Dop Sticks

These are nothing more than wooden dowels of various sizes. There are also metal dop sticks, but the wooden variety work just as well and are cheaper than their metal counterparts.

Metal Cabochon Stencils (templates)

These stencils are used to trace shapes onto the gemstone slabs, creating the outline for your cabs. The ones we recommend provide a good variety of shapes yet are simple enough to be well suited for beginning hobbyists. We recommend that you use double-layered templates, which have parallel stencil outlines on the top and bottom; these allow you to mark the selected shape onto the top or bottom of your slabs. These will give you a higher level of precision for cabs that you'll be finishing on both sides and makes some cabochon making processes easier.

Brass or Aluminum Stencil-Marking Pencils

Use these to mark the template outline onto the gemstone slabs. You can also use fine-point permanent markers as a substitute.

 **Methyl Alcohol**

This is used to "super-clean" your trim-cut cabochons before attaching them to the dop stick with dop wax. The alcohol removes all traces of oils (including oil from your hands) and saves you a lot of time having to re-dop your stones if they break free while sanding or polishing.

 X-Acto Knives

These can be used to shave off any excess dop wax from your cabochons before you start to grind or sand them. The dop wax can clog up your diamond discs, making them less effective.

Getting Started

Cabochon Making Reference Chart

STEP	MACHINE	CHAPTER
1. Stencil Shape onto Slab	n/a	n/a
2. Cut to Rough Shape	Trim Saw	Cutting, pg 71
3. Clean the Stone	n/a	n/a
4. Dopping	Dop Pot	n/a
5. Grind to Final Shape	Lapidary Sander	Face Polishing, pg 87
6. Chamfering	Lapidary Sander	Face Polishing, pg 87
7. Doming and Polishing	Lapidary Sander	Face Polishing, pg 87
8. Remove Cab from Dop Stick	n/a	n/a
9. Routing or Drilling (optional)	Lapidary Router or Lapidary Drill	Routing, pg 111 Drilling, 119
10. Tumble Polishing (optional)	Tumbler	Tumble Polishing, pg 45

Step 1: Stencil Shape onto Slab

Before starting, take note that we're assuming that you've created or acquired rough gemstone slabs large enough to create one or more cabochons using your chosen stencil outline.

First, determine which side of your gemstone slab will be the top or outward-facing side for your finished cabochons. While some cabs are finished on both sides, most usually display one side, which we will refer to as the top side of the cabochon.

With the top side of the slab face-up, identify a section of your selected gemstone slab that has pleasing colors and patterns. Place your chosen stencil shape over the top of the area you've picked out and move it around until you find a "sweet spot." Before beginning to mark the outline, consider whether you will use the slab to make multiple cabochons. If so, you might draw some light outlines with a regular lead pencil and then move the template around to see whether you have enough space for a second shape. In general, you should leave at least $1/2$" between your stenciled shapes. If you're

trying to get the most that you can out of expensive gemstone materials, you can try going closer, but if there's not enough space for trimming and grinding, you'll potentially risk ruining both cabochons.

Now it's time to use your metallic pencil or a fine-point permanent marker to mark the outline on the slab. The point of the pencil should be angled outwards; this ensures the stencil shape is marked cleanly. If you have a double-layered stencil, flip the stone over and mark the shape on the back of the slab.

Next, use a ruler or straightedge to mark a rectangular pattern that is approximately $1/4$" outside of the borders of the stenciled shape. Then, draw another rectangular pattern turned at a 45-degree angle to the first rectangle; these lines should be $1/4$" outside of the stenciled shape as well. (The lines of the second rectangle will "cut off" the corners of the first rectangle.) These will be your cut lines for trim sawing. It's best to extend the lines of these patterns past the corners somewhat, to help line up your trim-saw blade and make nice square cuts.

HELPFUL TIP: We strongly recommend that beginning lapidary artists start with basic, standard shapes, such as those available on the templates shown above. Nonetheless, we also encourage you to explore your creative instincts by designing your own patterns. Some of the most beautiful cabochons are in fact free-form, which means that they have been styled on the fly after starting with a general design pattern. Your love for making cabs will grow over time as you develop your own unique patterns.

Step 2: Cut to Rough Shape

Using a trim saw, cut along the lines of the rectangular patterns. To reduce the amount of wasted gemstone material, cut as close to the stenciled lines as possible. Since you are cutting from a flat slab, you won't need to use the rocking-and-rolling technique we taught you in slab and face cutting.

After you've cut along the lines you drew, there will still be a significant amount of excess material that should be cut away with the saw (rather than grinding it off); this is a big time saver. However, you should not cut closer than $^1/_{16}$" to the stencil outline.

As a final and optional part of this step, you can use the trim saw to cut a series of small notches around the rim of the cabochon (which will make it appear as if there are small teeth protruding from the shaped cabochon). This process makes the rough grinding activity go more quickly. However, we recommend that you only use this process after gaining some experience with using your trim saw. (**Note:** The saw blade will cut slightly farther into the cabochon on the bottom side than the top, so take extra caution to stop cutting slightly short of the stencil mark on the top side.)

Step 3: Clean the Stone

Clean the cabochon thoroughly so that it adheres firmly to the dop stick. We recommend that you use a cleaning agent, such as methyl alcohol, to remove all traces of oil left by the saw and any residue from your fingers.

Step 4: Dopping

Depending on the size of the cabochon, you need to decide whether to perform this step or skip ahead to Step 5 and hold the cab with your fingers during the grinding process. Most experienced cabochon makers invariably dop their cabs to save wear and tear on their fingertips. For smaller cabs (under an inch), as well as more delicate cabs, you should always perform dopping before grinding.

Heat up the dop wax in your dop pot. The wax should be melted but not boiling. While the wax is melting, warm the stones by setting them on the edge of the dop pot. Dip the dop stick into the wax and rotate it slowly while pulling the stick back up out of the wax. You should have a nice-sized glob of dop wax; allow it to cool slightly before pressing it down against the back (unstenciled) side of the stone. Set the stone facedown onto a flat surface, with the dop stick standing straight up from the stone (this ensures that the face of the stone and the stick are perpendicular to each other). (**Note:** Allow the wax to cool for at least five minutes before moving to the next step!)

Step 5: Grind to Final Shape

Mount your rough grinding disc on the lapidary sanding machine, turn the machine on, and start the water dripping, as described on page 100.

Press the edge of the rough cabochon against the disk and gradually rotate it around the circumference of the stone. At this point, you should grind right up to the stenciled outline.

Take a final "lap" around the circumference of the stone until all the excess material has been removed and the stencil outline is no longer visible.

Step 6: Chamfering

Chamfering is the first step in doming, which gives your cabochon that eye-pleasing surface. Your primary goal is to grind away excess material to create a beveled edge around the stone. This beveled edge is called a chamfer (or a top rim or girdle). The chamfer is important because it makes it much easier to give the cabochon its famous domed shape. (Chamfering is described in detail on pages 101–102.) The illustrations below show the progression of the cabochon through the three primary stages. The process starts with the flat cab as shown in the "start" figure.

Then, go all the way around the edge and sand off about 1-2 millimeters of stone while holding the stone at

start · chamfered · domed

about a 30-degree angle to the disc, as shown. This is done by pressing the corner of the face of the cab against the grinding disk and gradually rotating the cabochon all the way around.

Next, sand off the sharp inner edge all the way around so that it blends in with the top. This is done by gently rocking the top edge of the chamfer you just created against the grinding disk and rotating the cabochon around its circumference.

Step 7: Doming and Polishing

Rather than repeating the processes we discussed on pages 101–108 of the Face Polishing chapter, see those instructions for this step.

Since you already have a nicely shaped stone without surface flaws, and since you are working with a small, more delicate piece of gemstone material, you won't need to use the ultra-rough grinding disc (although you can use it to create the chamfer).

Your cabochon will be attached to a dop stick, making it easier to perform the more delicate operations that are required for cabochons. These three photos show how to hold and move your stone while it is attached to a dop stick, and they demonstrate the rocking motion necessary to create a domed surface (and to sand and polish it) and the rotating motion to use while rocking it.

You may choose to skip Stages 4–5 from the Face Polishing chapter (ultra-fine sanding and polishing) and instead perform these steps in a tumbler. If you are only doing two or three cabs, it's probably best to use the face polishing machine, as it is faster.

Step 8: Remove Cab from Dop Stick

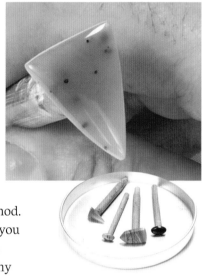

There are numerous ways to remove a cabochon from a dop stick, but the simplest and most reliable way is to set it in a pie plate in your freezer for about an hour. The cab will then either drop off on its own, or you can lightly pull it free from the dop wax. Some people soak the stone in methyl alcohol, and others will reheat the stone, but we don't recommend either method. Whichever method you choose, you may need to use an X-Acto knife or a razor blade to scrape away any remaining bits of dop wax.

Step 9: Drill or Rout the Cabochon (optional)

If you want to rout or drill your cabochons, these steps are covered in the Routing (page 111) and Drilling (page 119) chapters. Routing or drilling should be performed before tumble polishing your cabs.

Step 10: Tumble Polishing (optional)

Most experienced lapidary artists use a tumbler for the final polishing steps of cabochon making. It is simply done for efficiency; for example, if you have 10 or more cabochons, you'll get more cabs done with less effort by using the tumbler. One other nice benefit of using the tumbler is that it polishes both sides of the cabochon. See the Tumble Polishing chapter (page 45) for instructions.

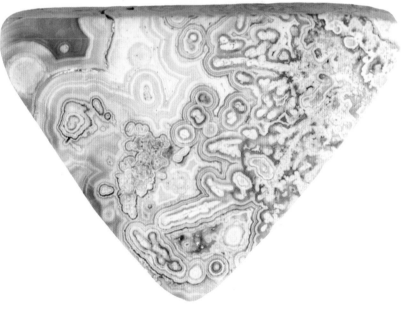

An Introduction to Styles and Techniques

There are nearly as many jewelry styles as there are types of gemstones, and it would be beyond the scope of this book to try to cover them all. But we would like to provide a brief introduction to the variety of jewelry making styles and techniques, and we hope it whets your appetite for creating your own jewelry designs. (See Recommended Reading for Jewelry Making on page 170 for a list of publications providing detailed instruction.)

This chapter introduces you to eight different processes for creating necklace jewelry, and for each process, the possibilities are endless. Stones, shapes, sizes, findings and chains are all variables, not to mention the many types of jewelry in addition to necklaces, such as earrings, bracelets, bolos, belt buckles, etc. While it is impossible to cover every option, we intend to open your eyes to the many possibilities now that you have a tumbled, shaped, routed and/or drilled stone.

Our biggest tip to you is that jewelry styles and tastes are infinite and very personal. So start simple, and keep your gemstone materials in focus as you develop your own creations. As many lapidary artists say, "Let the stone lead you."

For inspiration, there are numerous websites that offer jewelry equipment, supplies and tutorials. You can also find help by visiting your local craft stores. Many offer day classes to get you started!

Cabochons in Bezel Settings

A bezel is a grooved ring made to encase a finished gemstone or other decorative item. Bezel settings may have a closed back, which is great for supporting your stone, or an open back, which allows light to pass through your stone. The term "bezel" refers to the "wall" around the edge of the setting. This wall sits about ¼" higher than the back of the setting, creating a cup in which to set your stone.

If you use a sized cabochon (by following the sizes on your template), you can purchase a bezel specifically sized to fit your stone. (This also makes it easy to create multiple pendants of the same size.) The simplest way to set a cabochon into a bezel is to attach it with a lapidary-grade adhesive.

Cabochons can also be set in a bezel by bending the bezel wall (or prongs, in some settings) down over the edge of the stone. This requires tools such as a bezel pusher or plastic mallet.

A more advanced technique is to make your own bezel settings, which will take tools and training in the silversmith field. But this allows you to make a cabochon of any non-standard size and shape you want, as you can make your own bezel to fit it. It entails measuring a bezel strip, cutting it to the size of your stone, soldering the ends together, and then soldering the bezel to a bezel plate.

JEWELRY PROJECT #1

Attaching a Cabochon with Adhesive

This project starts with a cabochon made by following the steps in the Cabochon Making chapter (page 133). A standard-size cabochon (made using your template set) is required, so that it will fit an equivalent-size setting. And it is important to use a cabochon with a flat back to ensure that the stone will adhere to the setting.

Tools and Supplies Needed

- A closed-back bezel cup pendant setting that matches the size of your cabochon (these will typically have an attached bail, to allow it to be hung on a necklace)

- Plastic or rawhide mallet

- Polishing cloth

- Methyl alcohol

- Epoxy 330 2-part adhesive

- Chain or other necklace

Step 1: Cleaning the Surfaces

To ensure a strong hold, the surfaces of the cabochon and the setting need to be clean and dry. Use a polishing cloth and a small amount of methyl alcohol to clean the cabochon, then let it dry thoroughly.

Step 2: Mix and Apply the Epoxy

Mix the epoxy according to package directions. When the epoxy is ready, apply a small amount to the back of the cabochon. It is best to put the epoxy in the middle of the stone and spread it out to the edges. Be careful not to get too close to the edge, however, as excess epoxy will spill over. (Use methyl alcohol to remove any excess.)

Step 3: Mount the Stone

Mount the stone into the bezel, tapping gently with a plastic or rawhide mallet if necessary to create a secure fit, then allow the epoxy to cure according to directions. (Don't shortchange the curing time.) Your finished piece is now ready to hang on a chain or necklace.

Cabochons in Clay Settings

Another way to attach a cabochon to a necklace without drilling into or through the cab is to bake your stone into a polymer clay or metal clay setting. Most cabochons will tolerate the low temperatures used for baking polymer clay. However, when using metal clay, it's imperative that you first check the survivability of your stone (gemstone firing charts are available online and in books on metal clay and jewelry making). This is both for your safety and the integrity of your stone.

Clay settings can be made by molding your medium and shaping it free-form or with a pattern. Many times multiple stones are set together, or jewels or other decorative items are set in with the stone. You may choose to imprint the clay with a stamp or design, and you can paint your clay with acrylic paint. (Use a sealer after baking if you decide to paint.)

Most polymer clays are baked at a low temperature in an oven; it is best to have a dedicated oven (or mini-oven) for baking clay. You can also bake the clay without the stone and attach the stone with a strong lapidary-grade adhesive after baking; if you do so, be sure to use the stone to make an imprint in the soft clay before baking, as this will provide matching surfaces and help in mounting the stone after baking.

Working with metal clay is an advanced technique, as the clay is fired with a flame torch or in a kiln. There are many books available on this subject for further reading.

JEWELRY PROJECT #2

Setting a Stone in Polymer Clay

To make this project, start with a cabochon made by following the steps in the Cabochon Making chapter (page 133).

Tools and Supplies Needed

- Clay roller
- Cookie cutter, or other form to make your desired shape
- 5-10 ounces polymer clay, your choice of color
- Acrylic paint and sealer, if desired
- Chain or other necklace

Step 1: Knead and Roll the Clay

Start with a small amount of clay and work it until it softens. Next, roll it to your desired thickness; 2-3 millimeters thick works best.

Step 2: Cut the Shape

Use your cookie cutter or other form to cut the desired shape.

Step 3: Set the Stone

Set the stone in the clay as desired. You may wish to add a decorative edging over your stone to ensure that it will stay in place. Make sure to also add a bail or opening for attaching your chain or necklace.

Step 4: Decorate

You may wish to enhance your piece by adding design elements, such as decorative imprints, acrylic paint, etc.

Step 5: Bake the Clay

Bake the clay, following the instructions on the polymer clay packaging. It is advised to used a dedicated oven for baking, as the clay will emit fumes that you won't want in your home oven. Allow your piece to cool completely. If you added any acrylic paint to your project, it is important to seal the paint after it has cooled. Hang from the necklace of your choice.

Face Drilled Stones and Jump Rings

A gemstone that has been face drilled (drilled through from front to back) is easy to attach to a chain or cord with the use of a jump ring. This techniques offers endless creative possibilities, from a single hole drilled through the center and top of a stone, to numerous holes and jump rings placed creatively on the stone.

JEWELRY PROJECT #3

Attaching a Jump Ring

This project requires a finished gemstone that has been face drilled as described in the Drilling chapter (page 119). (**Note:** Remember that it's best to drill the stone before the final sanding and polishing, as this will smooth out any imperfections created during the drilling operation.) For this project drill a hole through the stone that is slightly larger than the diameter of the jump ring wire.

Tools and Supplies Needed

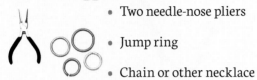

- Two needle-nose pliers
- Jump ring
- Chain or other necklace

Step 1: Open the Ring

Use two needle-nose pliers to grab the two sides of the ring on either side of the opening. Open the ring by twisting your wrists in opposite directions to make the ring open sideways, and not by pulling your wrists, and the ends of the ring, away from each other. (**Note:** This is important because it allows you to grip the ring very gently with the pliers; gripping too tightly will mar the surface.)

Step 2: Attach the Necklace

Slip the ring through your stone and over the chain of your choice. You can also use string, leather or ribbon. The options are endless.

Step 3: Close the Ring

Close the ring by twisting it shut with your pliers.

Headpins and Eyepins

A gemstone that can be drilled all the way through from top to bottom can be fitted with a headpin or eyepin. (**Note:** This technique works only for softer and smaller gemstones, as the amount of drilling required would be excessive for harder stones, such as agates.) Headpins have a closure at the bottom, and on the top they have wire that is used to create a bail. You can accessorize this by adding beads above or below the stone as desired.

JEWELRY PROJECT #4

Attaching a Headpin

This project begins with a finished gemstone that has been drilled through from top to bottom. Follow the top drilling instructions as described in the Drilling chapter (page 119). (**Note:** Remember that it's best to drill the stone before the final sanding and polishing, as this will smooth out any imperfections that are created during the drilling operation.) For this project, drill a 2-millimeter hole through the stone.

Tools and Supplies Needed

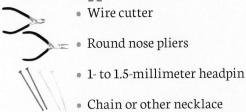

- Wire cutter
- Round nose pliers
- 1- to 1.5-millimeter headpin
- Chain or other necklace

Step 1: Insert the Headpin

Insert the headpin through the stone from the bottom to the top.

Step 2: Create the Bail

Using the pliers, create a loop in the wire and then wrap it back around itself to secure the end of the wire (this will take a bit of practice to learn). To attach a closed necklace, insert the chain or cord into the bail as you are creating it. Clip off any excess wire.

Top Drilled Stones and Upeyes

A gemstone that has been top drilled (drilled partway into the top of the stone) and then fitted with an upeye makes for a clean and simple presentation. Upeyes are available in a wide variety of designs and colors.

JEWELRY PROJECT #5

Attaching an Upeye

Start this project with a finished gemstone that has been top drilled as described in the Drilling chapter (page 119). (**Note:** Remember that it's best to drill the stone before the final sanding and polishing, as this will smooth out any imperfections that are created during the drilling operation.) It is advised to use a soft stone for top drilling.

For this project, drill a 2-millimeter-wide hole 4 millimeters deep into the stone.

Tools and Supplies Needed

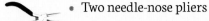

- Two needle-nose pliers

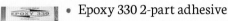

- 6 x 3-millimeter upeye with 1 millimeter post

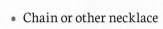

- Epoxy 330 2-part adhesive

- Methyl alcohol

- Chain or other necklace

- Jump ring

Step 1: Mix and Apply the Epoxy

Follow the instructions on the epoxy package to mix the two parts together. When the epoxy is ready to use, apply a small amount to the post of the upeye.

Step 2: Attach the Upeye

Slip the upeye into the hole in the stone and set the stone upright (upeye on top). Allow the epoxy to cure according to the instructions, allowing plenty of time (24–48 hours). Clean any residual epoxy from the stone with methyl alcohol.

Step 3: Open the Ring

Use two needle-nose pliers to grab the two sides of the ring on either side of the opening. Open the ring by twisting your wrists in opposite directions to make the ring open sideways, and not by pulling your wrists, and the two ends of the ring that meet each other, away from each other. (**Note:** This is important because it allows you to grip the ring very gently with the pliers while you open it; gripping it too tightly will mar the surface.)

Step 4: Attach the Necklace

Slip the ring through the upeye and over the chain of your choice. Close the ring by carefully twisting it shut with the pliers.

Side Drilled Stones (Beads)

Another option for softer stones is to drill a hole through from side to side, near the top of the stone, and then string a small chain, cord or string directly through the hole.

JEWELRY PROJECT #6

Stringing a Bead

Begin this project with a stone that has been side drilled. Follow the instructions for face drilling as described in the Drilling chapter (page 119), except, of course, drilling through from side to side, and not front to back. (**Note:** Remember that it's best to drill the stone before the final sanding and polishing, as this will smooth out any imperfections that are created during the drilling operation.)

Tools and Supplies Needed

- Needle-nose pliers
- Chain, cord, string or other necklace

Step 1: Stringing the Stone

String the necklace of your choice through the stone. You may need to use a needle-nose pliers to remove or adjust the ends of a chain in order to fit it through the stone. Be creative and include multiple stones and beads if you'd like.

Wire-Wrapped Tumbled Whole Stones

Wire wrapping is a great way to make beautiful jewelry out of tumbled whole stones, and the design can be as simple or as complex as you would like it to be. Simple is the best way to start, of course, but as your comfort and skills grow, you'll soon be taking on more intricate and creative projects. The possibilities are endless; one can find hundreds of tutorials online, for projects simple to ornate.

When it comes to selecting wire for your project, there are choices to be made about metal type (silver, bronze or copper, for example), shape (round or square), color, gauge and pliability of the wire. Shape and color are simply a personal choice, but keep in mind that some people are sensitive to different metals.

Wire gauge is critical (and remember, the lower the gauge, the thicker the wire). For smaller stones, we recommend 24–26 gauge wire. For medium stones, 20–22 gauge is optimal, as it will hold your stone more firmly. Sometimes you may want to wrap the wire as a single strand, and sometimes you may want to use double or triple strands of wire, or even braid three wires together first before wrapping the stone! Often two or three different types of wire are used in one project.

Wire comes in three levels of pliability—dead-soft, half-hard and full-hard. The softer the wire, the easier it will bend. For wire wrapping, dead-soft wire is usually preferred. Always polish your wire before beginning your project.

A good set of tools is imperative with wire wrapping. Pliers are used to bend and tighten the wire around your projects. Mandrels or dowels are used to make spirals and other decorations.

JEWELRY PROJECT #7

Making a Wire-Wrapped Pendant with a Whole Stone

One of the simplest wire-wrap design patterns that you will see follows the generalized set of steps below. This will give you a project that should take no longer than 15 minutes, even on your first try!

For this beginner project, it is best to begin with a medium-size stone (about 30–40 millimeters in width), as this will give you enough room to work with. (**Note:** As this is somewhat of an advanced technique, use the photo on page 160 for reference.)

Wire Wrapping Tools and Supplies

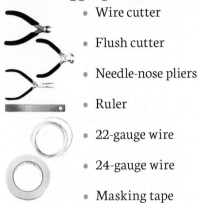

- Wire cutter
- Flush cutter
- Needle-nose pliers
- Ruler
- 22-gauge wire
- 24-gauge wire
- Masking tape

Step 1: Choose the Design and Wire

Wire wrapping, like most hobbies, is learned with practice, so start by deciding on a simple design. Pick a wire color and choose a wire thickness; for the medium-size stone in this project, use 22-gauge wire for wrapping and 24-gauge wire for securing your wrap.

Step 2: Measure and Cut the Wire

Measure the circumference of your stone and add 10 inches. Cut four pieces of 22-gauge wire to this length and lay them side by side. Next, cut one piece of 24-gauge wire 12 inches long. This will be used to tie the bundle of four pieces together at the bottom, sides and top. (You can start with this wire already cut into four pieces, but it is easier to hold if it is longer, so start with it full length and cut it as you go along.)

Step 3: Tape the Wires

Make the four pieces of wire into a bundle by wrapping them together with a small piece of masking tape. Place the tape close to the midpoint between the ends of the wires, but not exactly in the center, as the 24-gauge wire will be wrapped there. The tape will help keep your bundle together as you make your first wire wrap.

Step 4: Begin Wrapping

Wrap the 24-gauge wire around the midpoint of the bundle of four pieces; make six wraps and then clip the wire. This will be at the bottom of your pendant. Shape the four wire strands around the cabochon and wrap the strands together with 24-gauge wire on each side of the cabochon and at the top, to secure the stone.

Step 5: Continue Wrapping

Secure the cabochon in place by using the needle-nose pliers to bend the front-facing wire strand over the top of the cabochon at the top left and right corners and the bottom left and right corners. The result will resemble something of a cross-like figure over the front of the cabochon. Repeat this on the back-facing wire strand.

Step 6: Create a Bail

Bend the wires at the top into a small loop, and then wrap them together with a small piece of wire.

Step 7: Finish the Design

With the remaining wire at the top, you can create flourishes by winding the four strands into small concentric circles, if desired.

Wire-Wrapped Edge-Routed Stones

By using a router to create a groove around the perimeter of a gemstone, you can tightly wrap a thin wire around the stone that will be nearly invisible. The wire will stay securely in place around your stone, and since the wire is hidden, it will make for a simpler style, showcasing your stone and not the wire. (Of course, you can still make your project as elaborate as you wish.) This wire is then brought to a loop at the top, allowing you to attach a jewelry chain or cord.

A

Abrasive (or grit): A silicon carbide-based compound that is very hard and is used during tumbling to smooth out rough edges and prepare the surfaces of gemstones for polishing. There are multiple grit meshes that become successively finer as you progress through the tumbling stages.

B

Banding: A feature of some gemstones (primarily agates) of alternating color bands. The best banding features have striking contrasts from one color band to the next.

Bezel: A grooved ring made to encase a finished gemstone or other decorative item.

Burnishing: A final or secondary application of polishing compound in the face polishing process that is meant to bring out the highest gloss possible.

Burr: A protruding section of gemstone material left after cutting your stones in half or into slabs. No cut is ever perfect, but some leave a more noticeable burr to be cut or ground away.

C

Cab: Short for cabochon.

Cabochon: A piece of gemstone material that has been cut and ground into a pleasing and symmetrical shape, usually for jewelry making. It might be a standard shape, such as an oval or rectangle, or one that is handmade or crafted free-form.

Chamfer: A narrow beveled edge that is ground around the perimeter of a piece of gemstone material for the purpose of creating a sloped or domed surface. After creating a chamfer, subsequent grinding eventually removes the flat beveled edge and brings the surface of the gemstone to a smoothly contoured dome.

Cut slab: A thinly cut slice from a whole stone, such as agate, or from a piece of gemstone material, such as jasper or quartz.

D

Dendritic: Plant-like formations inside of various agate types, such as Montana moss agates. These formations can often be seen as natural scenes, such as birds, trees or hills.

Diamond polishing paste: Finely ground diamond mixed into a paste material that is spread onto face polishing discs. The diamond paste performs the polishing and burnishing of gemstones to a high-gloss shine.

Dome polished: Gemstones that have been shaped into a smoothly contoured surface, or dome, and then polished. This may be done to whole stones, stones that have had a portion of their surface cut away, or to gemstones formed into cabochons.

Doming: A set of steps starting with a rough or flat surface, creating a beveled edge, or chamfer, and then gradually removing surface material through a series of rocking and rotating motions using grinding and sanding discs coated with diamond abrasives.

Dop pot: A small electric heating pot that is specifically made to heat dop wax to just the right temperature for melting and then molding.

Dop sticks: Small wooden or metal dowel-like rods about 6 inches in length for attaching to gemstone pieces with dop wax. Dop sticks are used to help hold gemstones as they are shaped into cabochons.

Dop wax: A specially formulated wax that forms a super-tight bond between gemstone material and a dop stick. This tight bond is necessary so that the gemstones can be pressed against grinding, sanding and polishing discs without coming loose from the stick.

E

Extender fluid: A fluid that helps bind diamond polishing paste to the polishing disc. This helps to get more polishing done with a single application of the polishing paste.

Eyepin: See *headpin.*

F

Face: The surface of a stone that will be cut and/or polished. It is generally the most attractive surface, which exhibits the most color and pattern.

Faceting: Refers to any flat spots on a domed stone. These flat spots are visually unappealing and can result from pressing the stone against the grinding disk and holding it in one place without rocking or rotating.

Face drilling: When a cabochon or slice of a whole stone is laid flat and then drilled from front to back. The hole will go all the way through the stone.

Face polishing: Grinding, shaping and polishing one surface (the "face") of a whole stone and leaving the rest of the stone in its rough state. The surface to polish is the one that exhibits the most striking color and pattern.

Finding: See *jewelry finding.*

Flat lapidary sander: A machine that is used for grinding, sanding and polishing gemstone pieces using horizontal discs that spin at high speeds.

G

Girdling: Another term for chamfering. See *chamfer.*

Grit: See *abrasive.*

H

Headpin (or eyepin): A small metal jewelry post that goes all the way through a gemstone bead; a necklace or bracelet chain can be threaded through a circular eye at the top of the stone.

High-gloss finish: Otherwise known as a high polish, this is the final result of tumble polishing and face polishing. It can only be obtained through the careful practice of the processes described and the use of high-quality lapidary machines and supplies.

J

Jewelry finding: Any small metallic implement that is made for the specific purpose of attaching a gemstone pendant (such as a cabochon) directly to a necklace or bracelet chain or cord, or to a jump ring, which connects the finding and the chain.

Jump ring: A small metal ring that attaches to a jewelry finding on a gemstone pendant. A necklace chain or cord is then threaded through the jump ring.

L

Lapidary: A term used to describe a variety of processes, such as cutting, polishing, shaping and drilling gemstone materials for display or jewelry making.

Lapidary drill: A drill press made specifically for drilling very hard gemstone materials. Lapidary drills are different from carpentry drills in that they run at lower speeds and may be equipped with devices to spray lubricants onto the gemstone pieces and hold them in place while drilling.

M

Mohs hardness scale: A scale used to measure the relative hardness of gems and minerals, with 10 being the hardest (diamond), and 1 being the softest (talc). Most of the gemstones used in lapidary processes have a hardness between 6 and 8.

N

Natural-shape pendants: A thin slice of a whole gemstone that is polished and used for jewelry making. Smaller-size agates are the primary type of gemstones that are used for this purpose.

R

Rapid rinsing: A sub-process within the cleanup step for vibratory tumblers. Since vibratory tumblers are top loading, it is easy to pour water and a small amount of liquid soap into the tumbler and then run it for a short amount of time to help remove tumbling grit and polishing compound.

Rockhound oil/lapidary lubricant: A specially formulated mineral oil used for some lapidary saws to cool the saw blade, reduce the amount of rock dust that could be breathed in and keep stones from being excessively scratched and fractured while sawing.

Rotary tumbler: A type of lapidary machine used for tumble polishing stones. The tumbler barrel for rotary tumblers lays horizontally on the base of the machine. The contents inside the barrel gently tumble over each other and gradually smooth and polish the gemstone materials.

Rough cut: Rough cutting simply means cutting away excess material from gemstones for face polishing or cutting gemstones into slabs or slices.

Router: A lapidary machine used to cut a shallow groove around the outside of a gemstone pendant or cabochon; a thin wire can then be fit inside the groove and brought together with a small loop at the top of the stone.

S

Satin finish: A semi-gloss finish on gemstone materials. This is an alternative to a high-gloss or polished finish and is less labor-intensive to achieve than polishing.

Silicosis: A serious health condition that results from breathing in excessive amounts of rock dust. You can nearly eliminate the risk of silicosis by using lubricants when cutting and grinding, and keeping a ventilation fan running in your work area; you can also wear a dust mask or respirator.

Sintered: Sintered lapidary saw blades feature a narrow strip of crushed diamond particles that are bonded to the blade. This narrow strip of diamond does all the cutting work.

Slabbing: A lapidary term used to describe the cutting of gemstone material into thin slices. These slices might be from whole or natural-shape stones (such as agates), or they might be from chunks of stone (such as petrified wood or jasper).

Stages (in polishing): For tumbling and face polishing there are multiple stages that bring gemstones from rough material to a satin finish or a high-gloss polish. Within each stage there is a set of repeating steps.

Stencil: For lapidary purposes, these are thin metallic sheets that have numerous symmetrical shapes (such as oval, circle, diamond). The stencils we recommend are two-layered, so that you can draw a shape on both sides of a slice of gemstone material. These shapes will be cut and ground into polished cabochons.

Steps (in polishing): For tumbling and face polishing there are sets of repeating steps within the overall stages. Process steps also occur in the other chapters, but the word "steps" takes on this unique meaning in the Tumbling and Face Polishing chapters.

T

Top drilling: When a hole is drilled partway into the top of a gemstone so that a jewelry post can be glued into place, and then attached to a necklace or bracelet.

Top loading: Vibratory tumblers sit upright. As such, rocks and water can be put directly into the top of the machine. This is especially useful during the cleaning step of each tumbling stage.

Trim saw: A term used to describe lapidary saws. This often leads to confusion about whether separate saws are needed for cutting gemstone slabs and for making the finer trim cuts needed for cabochon making, but the saws we recommend in this book can and should be used for both purposes.

Tumble polisher: See *rotary tumbler.*

Tumble-polished: Any gemstone materials that have been processed through a series of tumbling stages to produce high-gloss or satin-finish gemstones for display and jewelry making.

Tumbling abrasive (or grit): A silicon carbide-based compound that is very hard and is used within tumbling processes to smooth out rough edges and prepare the surfaces of gemstones for polishing. There are multiple grit meshes, and successively finer grits are used as you progress through the tumbling stages.

Tumbling media: Small pellets that may either be ceramic or small pieces of gemstone materials that are used within tumble polishing processes to help carry the abrasives and polishing compounds; they also buffer the collisions of gemstones during the tumbling process.

U

Upeye: A small metal jewelry post with a circular hole or eye at the top. The post is glued into a hole that has been drilled into a cabochon, and then a necklace or bracelet chain can be run through the eye hole.

V

Vibratory tumbler: A type of lapidary machine used for tumble polishing stones. The tumbler barrel for vibratory tumblers sits upright. The vibrating motion of the barrel causes the contents inside the barrel to gently tumble over each other, gradually smoothing and polishing the gemstone materials.

W

Wire wrapping: A popular jewelry-making technique that involves wrapping thin wire made of copper, silver, brass or gold around polished gemstone pendants or cabochons. There is an endless variety of styles, from easy to very complex and intricate.

Recommended Reading for Jewelry Making

Lareau, Mark. *Getting Started Making Metal Jewelry.* Interweave Press, 2013.

Bombardier, Jodi. *Weave, Wrap, Coil: Creating Artisan Wire Jewelry.* Interweave Press, 2010.

Dascalu, Yonat. *Polymer Clay: All the Basic and Advanced Techniques You Need to Create with Polymer Clay.* CreateSpace, 2012.

Young, Anastasia. *Gemstone Settings: The Jewelry Maker's Guide to Styles & Techniques.* Interweave Press, 2012.

Miller, Sharilyn. *Bead on a Wire: Making Handcrafted Wire and Beaded Jewelry.* North Light Books, an imprint of F+W Publications, Inc., 2005.

McIntosh, Jim. *Wire Wrapping: The Basics and Beyond.* CreateSpace, 2007.

Soukup, Edward J. *Jewelry Making for Beginners: The Scroll Wire Method.* Gembooks, 1981.

French, Bernada. *Jewelry Craft Made Easy.* Gembooks, 1986.

Branson, Oscar T. *Indian Jewelry Making.* Rio Nuevo Publishers, 2000.

Jenkins, Fern and Viola Thrasher. *How to Make Wire Jewelry— Simple but Elegant.* Gem Guides Book Company, 2011.

Quality Lapidary Equipment Manufacturers

Tumblers
- Lortone
- Thumler's Tumbler
- Diamond Pacific
- Lot-O Tumbler
- Covington Engineering

Saws
- Lortone
- Hi-Tech Diamond
- Covington Engineering
- Diamond Pacific
- MK Diamond Products
- Barranca Diamond

Routers
- Gryphon

Polishers/Grinders
- Ameritool
- Hi-Tech Diamond
- Covington Engineering
- Lortone
- Diamond Pacific
- Inland

Drill Presses
- Vigor
- Covington Engineering
- Dremel
- Foredom

Index

Note: When a specific chapter is included, that page range is shown in bold for easier reference.

Index

M

Mary Ellen jasper, 21

Montana moss agate, 21, 79

moonstone, 21

N

natural-shape, 13, 25, 78, 81, 112–113, 117

O

obsidian, 21, 23, 36–37, 41, 64

ocean jasper, 21

P

petrified wood, 21, 23, 37, 40–41, 64, 78

picture jasper, 21, 28–29

polymer clay, 150–151

prairie agate, 21, 25

pricing for equipment and supplies, 15–16

R

rhodonite, 21

rockhound oil, 73, 77

rose quartz, 21, 34–35

rotary tumbler, 14–15, 45–69

routing/router, 14, 16, **111–117**, 163

S

safety, 75, 77, 81, 85, 92, 113, 150

satin finish, 53, 63, 68, 107

saw blades, 71, 75–77, 85

sea glass, 21

silicon carbide, 45, 49–50, 76, 122

silicosis, 75, 92, 113

slabbing, 71

smoky quartz, 21, 35

sodalite, 21, 31, 39

T

tiger eye, 21, 32–33, 64

top drilling, 119–120, 122, 124–125, 129, 156–157

trim saw, 14–15, 73–75, 137–140

tumble polishing, 15, 21, 24, 34, 40, **45–69**, 137, 144

tumbling abrasive, 49–50, 53, 57–62, 66–68

tumbling media, 15, 49–51, 57, 60–61, 66, 68

turquoise, 21, 42–43, 64, 103, 120

U

upeye, 156–157

V

vibratory tumbler, 14–15, 45–49, 56, 58–60, 63–65, 67–68

W

wire wrapping, 16, 111, 119–120, 160–163

173

Jim Magnuson

Rockhounding is more than a hobby for author Jim Magnuson—it's a serious and rewarding avocation that helps him connect with nature. He has been an avid hunter and student of various gems, minerals and fossils since his childhood, when he first began to hunt for stones in his native state of Illinois. In addition, Jim enjoys sharing his passion not only through showing and gifting some of his finds, but also through writing, another lifelong interest. Throughout Jim's career as an Information Technology professional, he has developed his technical writing skills while creating new processes that reduce complexity and improve efficiency. These same skills proved to be invaluable when he wrote a guidebook for beginning agate hunters, a project that gave him the confidence to develop a guide to lapidary processes that can be readily used by beginner-to-intermediate hobbyists. Jim is also a member of the Minnesota Mineral Club, and enjoys attending other rock and mineral clubs as a way to further his learning and branch out into other types of agates, gemstones and geology.

Val Carver

Rocks and lapidary work are both a rewarding personal avocation and a profession for Val Carver. While he is both educated and established as a practicing Chemical Engineer, his life has been centered around rocks, gems and minerals for the past 20 years, including ownership of a first-class lapidary supply and rocks, gems and jewelry business in Princeton, MN (Minnesota Lapidary Supply and Rocks & Things). This is not to say that Val has abandoned his engineering background and training, because he has continually leveraged that expertise to develop innovative lapidary tools and processes. It has also enabled him to work closely with lapidary wholesalers to both develop and procure high quality and economical lapidary tools and supplies. Val is always looking for ways to help his customers achieve success and satisfaction with their rockhounding and lapidary areas of interest, and he takes personal time to consult with them as they explore and learn some new machine, tool or process. Val's direct style helps hobbyists at all levels to skip through "layers of frustration" that often occur in the early learning stages. He has given the same energy and focus to helping create this book for lapidary hobbyists so they might experience the same personal rewards that he enjoys.

Carol Wood

Carol Wood took up professional photography as a means of satisfying a lifelong passion for creating and sharing things of beauty. She has a keen eye for seeing perspectives in things that on the surface appear to be mundane or quite simple. Given her training and natural instincts for perspective and complementary lighting that enhances visual clarity, Carol is able to produce high-definition photographic images that enhance but don't distract from the given subjects. These skills are essential in providing a guidebook that lapidary hobbyists can use as a just-in-time visual reference guide. In addition to Carol's photographic pursuits, she also enjoys outdoor activities with her friends and family, especially activities that have both a mental and physical component. As a result, she has become an avid rock hound and has gradually built a collection of beautiful agates that adorn her home in northern Illinois. Carol has also developed a personal interest in making jewelry pieces using gemstones she has found, and thereby has become familiar with many of the lapidary tools and processes in this book. Carol would have a hard time choosing between the joy of finding a beautiful gemstone and that of completing a lovely new jewelry piece!